The Anxious Parents' Guide to Quality Childcare

The
Anxious Parents'
Guide to Quality
Childcare

AN INFORMATIVE, STEP-BY-STEP MANUAL
ON FINDING AND KEEPING THE
FINEST CARE FOR YOUR CHILD

Michelle Ehrich

A PERIGEE BOOK

A Perigee Book
Published by The Berkley Publishing Group
A division of Penguin Putnam Inc.
375 Hudson Street
New York, New York 10014

Copyright © 1999 by Michelle Ehrich
Book design by Pauline Neuwirth, Neuwirth & Associates, Inc.
Cover design by Charles Björklund
Cover photo © by Stephen Simpson/FPG International

First edition: August 1999

Published simultaneously in Canada.

The Penguin Putnam Inc. World Wide Web site address is
http://www.penguinputnam.com

Library of Congress Cataloging-in-Publication Data

Ehrich, Michelle.
    The anxious parents' guide to quality childcare : an informative,
step-by-step manual on finding and keeping the finest care for your
child / Michelle Ehrich. — 1st ed.
        p.   cm.
    Includes index.
    ISBN 0-399-52515-7
    1. Childcare. 2. Caregivers. 3. Childcare services—
Evaluation. 4. Day-care centers—Evaluation. 5. Parent and child.
I. Title.
HQ778.5.E35   1999
362.71'2—dc21   99-26804
                                                                CIP

Printed in the United States of America

10 9 8 7 6 5 4 3 2 1

To my husband, Andy, who has always been so supportive and really does his fair share; to my children, Sam and Adam, who have changed my life only for the better; and to Mary Ann and Christy, for toilet training and so many other acts of love and patience.

CONTENTS

CONTENTS

CONTENTS

CONTENTS

PART III: KEEPING QUALITY CHILDCARE

APPENDICES

ACKNOWLEDGMENTS

This book would not have happened without the help and support of the following people: my husband and children, who are the real genesis of this book; Andy Zack, the first person in the publishing industry who believed in this project and me, and Sheila Curry, who then agreed with him; Mel and Paula, who raised me to believe that I would never fail; Jimmy V., who shared his knowledge of insurance; Gerry R., who knows all that tax stuff; and lastly, my many co-workers and friends who were there to commiserate and share their tales of childcare successes and failures.

Before You Start . . .

B EING A WORKING parent means that you work *two* jobs: one to earn a paycheck and the other to ensure that your children are safe, happy, and loved while you are doing the first job. The definition of a working parent is incomplete unless you include the words "one who dreams of finding and keeping high quality, reliable, suitable childcare." As working parents, our productivity at our paycheck job, indeed our very sanity, is absolutely dependent upon our success in solving the childcare question.

Parents can quickly and easily find someone to look after their child. The real challenge for working parents arises when they add the following modifiers to their childcare search:

High Quality
Reliable
Suitable

It is not always easy but it is very possible to do this successfully. I have and so have many other parents. During

1

my childcare searches, I learned that finding the "right" caregiver and arrangement requires much more than just good intentions and luck. It requires an understanding and awareness of your present and potential needs as well as a systemic approach to evaluating and making your choices. Think of the amount of time, energy, and research you devote to buying a car, a house, or perhaps a wedding dress. The search for childcare is weightier and more emotional, thus deserves at least as much of your devotion.

Childcare is an important and challenging job, especially when it involves *your* children. Finding the right person to fill that job cannot be accomplished in one day. If you wish to find quality childcare, you must be willing to devote your resources on all fronts: in preparation, in searching, and finally, in managing the caregiver relationship. Keep a positive attitude and remember that you have the ultimate in worthwhile goals: to find the "right" caregiver and arrangement to make your child feel loved and safe while you are earning your paycheck.

This book does not present an easy fix or magic solution, nor will it present you with the "right" caregiver for your child. Instead, you will find the tools to plan and conduct a productive childcare search and then build a strong relationship with the caregiver. The first two sections cover Preparation and Action and provide guidance on finding the caregiver and arrangement best suited to your family's needs. The final section presents information on the often overlooked and unanticipated issues that arise once you have made your childcare selection (Keeping Quality Childcare). In each section, there is advice designed to help you navigate smoothly through this process. I will also share some of my own experiences and opinions on childcare.

While the advice contained in this book is not foolproof, it will help you avoid the common pitfalls in the search for childcare: lack of preparation, lack of focus, strategic missteps, and decision making induced by panic. I explain how to identify candidate qualifications and job requirements methodically, and then discuss various childcare options (advantages, disadvantages, and price ranges) so that you can choose the most appropriate childcare arrangement to fit the needs and budget of your family. The book will explain how to identify productive search resources so that you can begin an efficient and targeted search. Once you have completed these preparations, you will find guidance on how to screen and interview potential candidates and how to check references, including ideas for questions to ask and suggestions on technique. You will find counsel on evaluating the finalists and making your choice. Finally, there are some parting suggestions for maintaining a satisfactory relationship with your child's caregiver. You may find that much of this is common sense and intuitive; however, in a situation involving your children, it is very easy to react emotionally. The objective of this book is to help you, the parent, to stay on track and find quality childcare without losing your mind.

As a working mother for more than seven years, first of one boy, then of two (Sam and Adam), my first lesson was that finding childcare was a more challenging undertaking than I had ever imagined. I quickly discovered that there was no comprehensive "guide" to doing this the way that I intuitively knew it should be done, and more disappointingly, there were no secrets to a fast success. Still, I had no choice but to forge ahead. My results were ultimately successful: I located two truly wonderful caregivers who were each with us for extended periods. First, I found a wonderful family day-care provider who cared for my boys for four years. When the transportation got to be too draining after a particularly harsh winter of moving two young children, and the boys' schedules became more demanding, we found a nanny who lived with us and cared for my boys for three years. The tools I identified and developed to find the best qualified caregiver to meet my family's needs can be applied to the unique needs and situations of all working families.

MAKING PEACE WITH YOURSELF: ACCEPTING YOUR NEED TO FIND CHILDCARE

Before you begin your search, you need to come to terms with some facts of working parenthood:

- You want and/or need to work.
- The caregiver may be with your child more than you are.
- Even the best caregiver will not do everything exactly your way.
- In a successful childcare arrangement, your child should love the caregiver. (Important note: This is *good*. You *want* this to happen. *Do not become jealous!*)
- This search may take a lot of your time, emotional commitment, and financial resources.
- You are trying to fill a very important and difficult job. The person who fills it deserves your highest respect.

It is *very* normal to feel that it is scary to look for childcare—it is a process fraught with emotions. Finding childcare means that you will be giving up some of your direct influence and supervision of your children and trusting someone else with these tremendous responsibilities. Feelings of guilt may lead many parents unwittingly to sabotage their own search efforts and fail to find the quality childcare they are seeking. You must make peace with yourself by accepting that you are a working parent and need to hire childcare. The task of finding good childcare will become infinitely easier once you have genuinely accepted your underlying reasons for doing so. By not agonizing over *why* you are looking for childcare, you free yourself to focus your energy on the real issues: What do I really want in a childcare situation, and how can I get it? Until you have passed this hurdle, you will have a very tough time trying to fill the position you are offering. Before you can start your search, you need to let go of the guilt and accept that you are doing what needs to be done.

KNOW YOUR PARENTING PHILOSOPHY

Before you begin your search, take a few moments to outline in writing the basic components of your Parenting Philosophy. This will serve as an important touchstone during the preparation process as you identify the type of person and arrangement best suited to your childcare needs. Your philosophy will also come in handy during the actual search when you interview candidates and visit childcare sites. The following is the Parenting Philosophy that my husband and I composed:

- Childhood should be fun.
- Children should be secure in knowing that they are unconditionally loved.
- Say yes whenever possible. When you say no, make sure you mean it.
- Choose your battles carefully . . . not everything is worth a fight. Avoid winning the battle but losing the war.
- Admit when you are wrong, and apologize.
- No physical discipline.
- You are the adult and you are in charge; ultimately the children know this, so you don't have to prove it.
- Children are like sponges; they hear and see everything, so be careful of what you say or do even when you think they are not watching.
- Always remember that you are a role model.

- Treat the child with the same respect you would want to receive.
- Obedience can be demanded; respect must be earned. As a parent, I would rather be respected.
- You cannot "control" a child. You *can* influence a situation, guide behavior, elicit cooperation, and suggest a path.
- Encourage independence and creativity.
- Praise the child for doing good things; positive reinforcement is the best form of discipline.
- Build the child's self-esteem and self-confidence.
- It is more important to try your best than to succeed.
- Getting dirty is okay—it all comes off in the wash.

By putting these thoughts on paper, it gave us greater focus and helped us to decide on which points we could compromise and on which we simply could not. The Parenting Philosophy is an excellent springboard for the beginning of your search.

PART I

Preparation

The Perfect Person: Defining Candidate Qualifications

WHEN DECIDING *WHO* you want to be your child's caregiver, you need to think about personality, temperament, skills, beliefs, etc. This step is distinct from that in which you determine *what* you want the caregiver to do and *when* (i.e., the Job Requirements), a topic that is covered in the next chapter.

The caregiver will be spending a great deal of time with your child; not only do you want to determine that she can provide quality care, you also want to ensure that she is a worthy role model and someone your child can love. You must be open-minded, recognizing that no single person can incorporate *all* the traits you seek. You must be prepared to decide what are the most important traits on which you will *not* compromise and on which you will. I believe that it is easier to compromise on "Skills" (e.g., speaks three languages, plays the piano) than on "Personality" requirements. The key is to be realistic—you are looking for a loving, child-oriented person with good common sense to help raise your child, not to raise the next Nobel Prize laureate or Olympics winner.

You can be as specific as you want in defining the Candidate Qualifications. For example, if you have a child with special needs, you may want someone with training or experience in this area. Just remember that as you become more specific in your Candidate Qualifications, especially in "Skills," you may need either to compromise more or to accept a more narrow range of candidates. You will miss out on some prospective candidates who are very strong on all the fundamentally important qualities you seek if you confine your search to those who may meet each specific qualification but none in an outstanding fashion. I had a former colleague who wanted to only see candidates who could play a musical instrument *and* had taken some college classes. She had her reasons for wanting these skills but these unique requirements caused her to miss seeing many otherwise strong childcare providers who would have done a great job with her children. Another co-worker felt that only another mother could care for her children in the way that she expected. Because she wanted a live-in nanny, this meant that she had to confine her search primarily to women who had grown children. As a result, her potential candidate pool was quite limited although because this was so important to her, she was comfortable with her decision not to compromise on this point.

If you are having a difficult time defining those qualities you are looking for in a childcare provider, your Parenting Philosophy can offer inspiration and ideas.

WHAT WE DID

We sought our first caregiver for Sam before my scheduled return to work when he was just ten weeks old. Our Candidate Qualifications were quite simple and focused on a short list of personality characteristics and skills that we felt were essential. I believe these are the foundation characteristics of a childcare provider:

CHILDCARE PROVIDER QUALIFICATIONS

Personality

1. Loving and patient
2. Cheerful
3. Child and family oriented
4. Good common sense (e.g., safety, driving, discipline, etc.)

Skills

5. Experienced in caring for infants (in our case, but always with children)
6. Checkable references. This may be one of the most important parts of any childcare search. You must *always* check references. Please refer to chapter 7 (page 101) for details on this vital step.

Because our needs were simple and our list was so short, there was nothing on which we would compromise as we searched for the right person. After several months of searching that began when I was still pregnant, we found a caregiver who met our Candidate Qualifications. She was a young mother of two, who clearly loved children and had already cared for others in addition to her own.

A few years later, as we began to look for a live-in nanny to care for our two boys, aged four years and eighteen months old, we had a much more complicated job to fill, and thus formulated many more candidate requirements. Not only would this person be our childcare provider, she would also be assisting in the smooth functioning of our household, *and* living with us. Moreover, as we became more experienced as working parents, our expectations evolved to include caregiver qualifications such as a knowledge of first aid. While the essence of our Candidate Qualifications remained the same, we added many more details. This meant that the likelihood of compromise on some points was far higher.

The following list is what we came up with for our live-in nanny. None of these qualifications is unique or overly specific although finding most of all of them in one person was a challenge.

CHILDCARE PROVIDER QUALIFICATIONS (LIVE-IN)

Personality

1. Love of children and desire to care for them
2. Positive attitude and outlook
3. Good judgment, patience, and common sense
4. Energetic and enjoys interacting with children (e.g., actively playing with them)
5. Well spoken
6. Creative
   WHY: Each of these qualifications is a basic and essential personality trait of the person who will be spending a lot of time with our children as they became more active. Since the childcare would be in our home, there would not be other children immediately available as playmates. We want someone who will be a good influence as well as fun to be with.

Skills

7. Prior childcare experience. Childcare training (e.g., nanny certificate) is a welcome credential.

WHY: This requirement reflects our concern that the caregiver is seeking a job that is enjoyable for her; a happy childcare provider makes for happy children. Also it was important to us that the childcare provider knew and understood how challenging it could be to watch two young children for twelve hours at a stretch. We wanted to eliminate anyone who thought this would be an easy job.

8. Prior paid work experience (either childcare or other)
9. Solid work ethic; willing *and* able to take and follow instructions
   WHY: These two latter requirements reflect our desire to find someone who understands what is needed to keep a job. It is also the description of someone who enjoys working.
10. Some first aid knowledge
11. Willing *and* able to do small errands and household chores for the family (including parents); basic cooking skills
    WHY: We wanted someone to help us out so that we could enjoy our weekends and evenings more; it was very important to be direct about this since some childcare providers will not do these tasks.

Other

12. No smoking
13. No drug use or alcohol abuse, past or present
14. Good health and grooming (this does not mean dressing as a fashion model but rather having a neat presentation that shows a degree of self-respect)
15. Clean driving record (and valid driver's license) and no police record
16. Experience in heavy suburban driving is a plus
17. High school graduate and some college or nanny courses

WHY: These are our general expectations of someone who we would permit to be with our children every day. They demonstrate "clean living" and intelligence.

18. Lived away from home for at least three months
19. Compatible personality/temperament with parents/ employers
   WHY: After looking long and hard for a quality live-in nanny, we did not want to lose her to homesickness or a personality conflict with my husband or me.
20. Checkable references: three work references (at least two childcare); two personal references (nonfamily); family references (parents and/or children)
   WHY: This point is so important it bears repeating: Checking references may be the **MOST IMPORTANT** part of choosing the right person to watch your child. **You must always personally check references** (refer to chapter 7 on references for advice).

Following a six-month preparation and search process, we were successful in hiring a very well-qualified nanny who cared for the boys for three years. We compromised on the following points: (10). some first aid knowledge, and (11). basic cooking skills.

DEFINING YOUR OWN CANDIDATE QUALIFICATIONS

Now you can begin to define your own Candidate Qualifications. Make two columns on a page, heading one "Personality/Temperament" and the other "Skills." Write down some of the personality traits that you feel are fundamentally important in any childcare provider. Next, focus on identifying additional attributes that would be specifically relevant to caring for your children (placing these in either the Personality or the Skills columns). For example, if you have a pool at your home, swimming ability may be an important skill; if your child loves to draw and paint, someone who is artistic may be appropriate. Clearly, specific skills are a very important consideration if your child has any special needs. A child with a hearing loss may need a caregiver who is fluent in American Sign Language; a child who has limited mobility may require a caregiver who is physically strong enough to assist with movement all day long; a child with a speech impediment may need a caregiver who speaks English without an accent to serve as a solid speaking model. After you have laid the basic groundwork, list some of the other skills that you think would be nice (or vital) to find in a qualified candidate who would be working with your child.

As you formulate the Candidate Qualifications, talk to other parents who have had experience in looking for and employing childcare providers. Ask what they thought were the strongest and weakest points of those providers they hired. Learn from both their successes and failures. If the employee worked out (or did not work out), try to find out what went right (or wrong). Our qualification of having lived away from home came from listening to three or four parents talking about losing their nannies to homesickness; the qualification of prior childcare experience reflected not only common sense but the secondhand tale we heard of a family who hired someone straight out of school who had never done more than occasional evening baby-sitting and decided she simply did not like being with young children all day.

Another way to approach this exercise is to think about people who have spent time with your child (or other children you know). Ask yourself what made you feel comfortable or uncomfortable about the way they interacted with the children. Once you have completed listing all the qualifications, identify those on which you may be willing to compromise. Looking at our qualifications for a live-in nanny, we might have compromised on previous paid employment for someone who had either taken childcare courses or had come from a large family, or we might have accepted someone who had never lived away from home if the person seemed mature and confident in other respects. Chances are good that you will have to compromise on at least one or two items, so it is useful to think about this matter before you start to screen candidates.

CHAPTER 3

What Do We Need?
The Job Requirements
and
the Job Description

B Y COMPLETING THE Candidate Qualifications in the preceding chapter, you have an idea of the type of person
you hope to have care for your child. In this chapter, you
will undertake two steps: *identify what you want the caregiver/
childcare arrangement to do* (which are the Job Requirements)
and then *structure the job* (which is the Job Description) by
including compensation and benefits. The first of these two
steps is applicable to both in-home and out-of-home
childcare arrangements; the second is more applicable to
in-home childcare arrangements. By completing this exercise, you will be better equipped to select the most appropriate childcare arrangement for your needs (as discussed
in the next chapter).

At the end of this chapter, there are a series of questions
that will help you identify the various elements of your
Job Requirements and Description. Be as thorough as
possible. Recognize and avoid the temptation of demanding more of your surrogate than you would of yourself in the same situation. For example, when you are

home with your infant, do you have the time to clean your entire home from top to bottom? Also, if you find that your job requirements contain more household assistance elements than childcare items (which may be the case if you have children who are in school all day), think carefully about whether you might need a housekeeper rather than a childcare provider.

You may be as specific as you wish in defining the job. However, by being overly specific or otherwise unrealistic you may eliminate many well-qualified candidates from consideration. I have an acquaintance who wanted in-home childcare so that she could also have some help with chores and errands. However, since she was a teacher and did not work in the summer, she wanted to furlough the childcare provider during that time. This may have been a reasonable job requirement in her mind but, since many childcare providers need a steady income, her position was unattractive to most potential candidates. She effectively limited her candidate pool to mostly mothers of school-age children who also wanted the summer off. It was a tough job to fill.

WHAT ABOUT BENEFITS AND COMPENSATION?

Caring for your child is basically your life and present destiny; however, for the caregiver, it is a *job*. Of course, it should be a very meaningful and enjoyable one for the caregiver, but it is still a *job*, which means that the person who does it needs to get a salary and perhaps other benefits. Your Job Description is not complete without mention of compensation and benefits to be offered to the childcare provider. The objective is to structure the compensation and benefits in a way that shows the caregiver that you recognize the importance of the job responsibilities and have a professional respect for her. Ultimately you are trying to get the most efficient use of your childcare dollars by finding the best quality caregivers for your budget. *You are not trying to find the cheapest (or most costly) childcare but rather the best.*

In the case of family or center-based day care, compensation is already set for you in the fees you are charged. If these fees are very low, it is a red flag that may signal that the caregivers are not being fairly compensated, are not well qualified, or not given the resources to do their jobs well.

Items included in compensation and benefits encompass:

- salary
- paid vacation and holidays
- use of car or car subsidy (for in-home care)
- living accommodations (if live-in)
- health insurance
- educational subsidies
- merit reviews and raises

For a day-care center, these benefits should be offered to the caregivers by the center itself. Ask the center director what is included in the compensation package. Even the best of centers may not have all these items. However, the absence of many of the above benefits may influence the quality of the staff that the center can attract and its turnover as its caregivers leave for more attractive and competitive compensation with other employers.

The cost of childcare can be strange. You can pay a lot and it might or might not buy the best-quality childcare available. However there does seem to be a strong correlation between paying a low price and poor-quality childcare. The best you can do is to assess what is the most that you would pay for your child's mental, emotional, and physical well-being. The most truthful answer to this query is that these things are priceless; you could never afford to *buy* them! Now look at your budget and decide how much you can afford to pay because these priceless things are what you are really trying to attain in your search for quality childcare. Give this point very careful thought as you formulate your childcare budget.

OUR JOB REQUIREMENTS

I found that the Job Requirements for our childcare provider changed over time as our situation and finances evolved. When Sam was a newborn and I was finishing my maternity leave, the Job Requirements for our childcare situation were fairly simple. They were so basic and commonsense that I believe with some personalization they should constitute the core of every family's childcare Job Requirements regardless of the type of arrangement that is ultimately selected.

1. A homelike environment, with a few children to form a "sibling" group (maybe two or three others) but where Sam was the only infant
   WHY: We wanted the setting to be as comfortable as a home (ours or another) and felt that a more institutionalized setting would not be as child friendly for an infant (clearly as a child enters toddlerhood, this changes). Also, because we were planning on having other children, we wanted Sam to be in an environment where he could be with other children, yet we did not want his needs as an infant neglected due to the demands of too many other infants. As we researched childcare arrangements in our area, this requirement led us to family day-care arrangements and away from more traditional day-care centers. In some communities however, the day-care centers also offer this homelike quality.

Moreover, the older the child, the less important this requirement may become for some families.

2. A loving and experienced childcare provider who met our Candidate Requirements

WHY: The most essential qualification for this job was to love children and understand their needs. We appreciated the fact that full-time childcare is a demanding job—it was important that the childcare provider also understood what was involved on a daily basis and had the background to deal with it appropriately.

3. Stability of the arrangement

WHY: We strongly believe that it is important for a young child to be in stable environment so that a positive and loving bond could be formed with the childcare provider. There are lots of horror stories about families who had several different childcare providers in the course of a year. Sometimes it was the fault of the family, sometimes of the provider. While we could not fully prevent such an occurrence, we wanted a childcare arrangement that was oriented toward consistency. We wanted prospective job candidates to know that we only wanted to speak with providers who were interested in establishing a long-term relationship.

4. Conformity to our work schedule

WHY: We both worked long (but not unheard-of) hours, with an especially early start of 6:30 A.M. We lived by the commuter train schedule, so we had no flexibility in the drop-off time; we could not risk having a childcare provider arriving even five minutes late for work because we would miss our commuter train. It was crucial that we found a provider who could reliably live with that requirement.

5. Conformity to our budget

WHY: We decided that the expense of quality childcare was not one on which we should try to economize. After covering the basics in our lives (mortgage, utilities, food), we were willing to spend what it took to get the best suitable arrangement that we could afford. If that meant no vacations or owning used cars, so be it. This was an investment in the well-being of our child. Remember that with very rare exceptions, you will get what you pay for in childcare.

Our first childcare search resulted in a family day-care arrangement. Every morning, we would bring Sam to a young mother's home in our town. She had two sons, a preschooler and first-grader, and was caring for an eighteen-month-old boy. Sam was exposed to other children in a homey, family environment that would offer stability in the caregiver, the setting, and the other children. When Adam was born two years later, the other child at the caregiver's home had left to begin a full day preschool so we could also bring Adam to the family day care as well.

Once Adam was a year old and Sam was three, we recognized that our Job Requirements had begun to evolve. The demands of waking and dressing *two* young children to bring to family day care in the predawn hours started to take a toll on us (especially after a harsh winter with five feet of snow). At the same time, Sam had started preschool and although the family day-care provider was able to transport him, the logistics of the situation did not allow him to enjoy enrichment classes, after-school play dates, or other types of activities. We also had to deal with having to choose between spending our ever-dwindling free time with the boys or doing our innumerable chores (such as food shopping, laundry, doctor appointments). It was a natural turn of events and we realized, to our sadness, that our situation had changed and, evidently, so had our childcare needs. The current family day-care arrangement no longer met all our updated Job Requirements. We sat down and revised our general Job Requirements to fit our new realities.

1. A loving and experienced childcare provider who met our Candidate Qualifications
   WHY: The very same reasons as before.
2. Stability of the arrangement
   WHY: The very same reasons as before.
3. Conformity to our work schedules
   WHY: The very same reasons as before.
4. Conformity to our budget
   WHY: We still could afford what we could afford. Happily, our circumstances had improved since we initially sought childcare: our incomes had risen and we had moved to a larger house. Both these factors meant that we could consider and, if desired, afford to have a nanny in our home.
5. Letting the children have an easier and more "normal" daytime routine (including sleep patterns and play dates)
   WHY: The early morning "up and out" was taking a toll on our children—especially Adam, who was a real "bedbug." If possible, we wanted the children to establish a more normal sleep/wake schedule. Moreover, the past winter had been particularly hazardous—if we could avoid taking the kids out in that kind of weather, we would. Lastly, now that Sam was getting older, he was developing friendships at preschool and wanted to have play dates, etc. We also thought it would be nice for Adam to enjoy some enrichment activities (play groups, toddler swim classes, etc.). None of this was practical if they were at the family day-care home.
6. Helping us so that we could enjoy more family time during our free time, meaning getting more chores/errands done for us while we were at work

WHY: We were learning by experience that the working parents of two children had expotentially less free time than the working parents of one child. Increasingly, our weekends were devoted to running errands and doing chores. If we could find someone to help with some of these chores during the week while we were at work, it would be heaven-sent.

OUR JOB DESCRIPTION

The Job Description that we formulated for our first childcare position (after Sam was born) was the same as our Job Requirements. All we really wanted was to find someone who could treat Sam with loving care in a child-friendly familylike environment and who could live with the reality of our long workday schedule and whose compensation was within our budget.

As our needs became more complex, so did our Job Description. The following is our comprehensive Job Description for in-home childcare; you will find that it is still fairly general in nature. The nanny employment contract (see page 130) can be even more specific if you desire.

THE EHRICH-ROSS FAMILY JOB DESCRIPTION

1. Primary responsibility: The children are your first and most important responsibility, everything else (e.g., laundry, dishes, etc.) is secondary. They need to be played with, read to, cared for while we are at work. We are looking for someone who will actively interact with our children and not just watch them. We hope that you will be a positive role model for our children, teaching them kindness, confidence, responsibility, and consideration.
2. General duties revolve around caring for our children while we are at work:

- Get children up and dressed in the morning; bathe them before we get home for dinner.
- Prepare children's breakfast and lunch and start family dinner; clean up kitchen after breakfast and lunch. On infrequent occasions when we have an evening engagement, you may be asked to prepare the children's dinner and clean up.
- Keep children's bedrooms and playroom neat.
- Drive children to school and other daytime activities and appointments (pediatrician, classes, play dates, sports programs).
- Play with children and plan activities during the day at home, in the yard, and with trips to park, library, shops in town, etc.
- Do local errands with children (including the grocery shopping, dry cleaners, etc.).
- Do limited and predefined household chores (family laundry, keeping house tidy).

3. Days and hours: We leave for work by 6:20 A.M. and return by 6:00 P.M. You are on duty when we are out of the house, even if the children are still asleep.
4. Tenure: We are seeking someone who, upon finding an enjoyable childcare position, is interested in staying for at least eighteen to twenty-four months.
5. Benefits: Negotiable, and includes competitive weekly salary, vacation, legal holidays, use of a car, and room and board.

The above description contained a very basic overview of a normal day/week for an in-home childcare provider working with our family. It was very direct in setting forth our general expectations (to be expanded upon in the employment contract discussed later) so that there would be no confusion once someone accepted the position. It also enabled candidates who were not interested in any of the identified tasks to eliminate themselves from consideration.

At this point, we were not specific about whether we wanted a live-in or live-out caregiver. As we did more research, we recognized that because our working hours began so early, a live-in caregiver was the optimal arrangement to suit our needs.

Please note that we broadly indicate the compensation and benefits associated with the position. We became more specific on this issue once we began to screen and identify viable applicants.

NOW IT IS YOUR TURN

Take a blank piece of paper and write down *everything* you ever wanted in the ideal childcare situation—along with your basic requirements and parameters (hours, salary, etc.). Refer to your Parenting Philosophy to make sure that you are structuring a job with which you are comfortable.

Now take another blank piece of paper and divide it into three columns headed:

1. *We must have this!*
2. I think this is also reasonable
3. When you wish upon a star . . .

Place each of the requirements from your first page into one of these three columns. To help make sure that you have covered many of the easily overlooked basics, take a look at the questions below and see if you have considered them. If you have missed something, be sure to put it on the list in the correct column. The point of this exercise is to be as specific as possible. *The better you define the job requirements, the better equipped you will be to identify the most suitable/best person and arrangement for you and your children.*

The following is a list of questions to help you get started in clarifying your Job Requirements and Job Description.

Your Basic Operating Parameters

This is an outline of your day, your need for flexibility, and your potential tolerance for childcare emergencies:

- I need to leave for work at_____. (Before I leave for work, I would like_____minutes to get ready without any interference.)
- My trip to and from work takes_____. There are/are not delays that sometimes arise due to traffic/public transit problems, etc.
- I will be home from work by_____. (When I get home, I need_____minutes alone to change clothes/regroup/sit down/return phone calls, etc.)
- I unexpectedly have to get to work early or stay late *never/ sometimes/often.*
- My job has the flexibility to accommodate emergencies at home, including child or caregiver illness. *Yes/No*
- My job requires me to travel on overnight trips. *Yes/No*
- My job requires me to work a flexible schedule (hours/ days/times).
- My partner has work commitments that are *more demanding than/less demanding than/the same as* mine.
- My partner's job requires travel on overnight trips. *Yes/ No*
- My partner's job requires working a flexible schedule (hours/days/times).
- My partner's job has the flexibility to accommodate emergencies at home. *Yes/No*
- My partner shares child-rearing responsibilities. *Yes/No*
- My partner shares household responsibilities. *Yes/No*
- We can afford to pay an inclusive total of $_____ *weekly/hourly.*
- We will give the following benefits (list): (car? paid vacation? health insurance? sick days? other?)

What Will My Kids Be Doing?

This section helps you to clarify what, where, and how you prefer to have your children spend their time while you are at work.

- I would like to see my children in an environment that is: (Fill in the general elements you wish for, such as "my home," "just like my house," "a clean day-care center," "with (or without) lots of other children," "spacious and stimulating," etc.)
- It is important to me that my children have a full schedule of planned activities. *Yes/No* (Such as?)
- It is important to me that my children are with other children during the day. *Yes/No*
- My children enjoy the following activities: (Fill in.)
- My children have the following schedules while we are working:
  - ➤ school: _____
  - ➤ lessons: _____
  - ➤ sports: _____
  - ➤ other: _____
- They will need transportation to these activities while with the caregiver. *Yes/No*
- They will need to be supervised while at these activities. *Yes/No*
- During the day, my children should accomplish the following:
  - ➤ finish homework
  - ➤ play outside
  - ➤ play inside
  - ➤ watch TV for_____ minutes/hours
  - ➤ play on the computer
  - ➤ have playdates
  - ➤ other: _____

- My children are not allowed to:
  ➤ always:
  ➤ most of the time:

Other Guideposts

- If possible, I would like someone to help me out at home by doing chores or errands such as: (list)
- I *am/am not* comfortable with someone else in my house. Living there?
- There are large/small/furry/_____pets in my home. *Yes/No*
  ➤ which do/do not require care. *Yes/No*
- I *do/do not* have an extra car/public transportation that the caregiver can use to transport my child.

These Job Requirements outline your fundamental childcare needs beyond those determined in your Candidate Qualifications. Contained within this section, you have determined: your childcare budget, the amount of flexibility you need and can tolerate in the arrangement, what the childcare environment should be like, and what activities and structure should be offered. The next step will be to understand what each of the many types of childcare arrangements do (and do not) provide as well as the costs of each one. This information will be assessed within the context of your Job Requirements, your Candidate Qualification, and lastly your resources, to assist you in selecting the arrangement best suited to your overall situation.

Selecting the Most Suitable Arrangement (Otherwise Known As Taking Your Reality Medicine)

ONCE YOU HAVE identified the Candidate Qualifications and the Job Requirements, you need to assess what type of childcare arrangement best meets those parameters. Before you start to make any concrete decisions, you need to keep in mind the following points.

1. *What can I afford to pay for childcare?*

Here is where you make a final determination of what you can and are willing to pay for childcare. My personal philosophy is that since this is a very important job, we are willing to pay top dollar to get the right person and arrangement. That means that we may settle for a cheaper car or vacation but we have made that choice. Review your budget *very* carefully and decide on a general cost range with which you are comfortable. Remember to keep your priorities straight.

2. *What are my key and most important candidate and job requirements?*

Focus on those requirements that absolutely will not

change. For example, we would not compromise on the requirement that the childcare provider has previous experience. If you live near the water, you may feel that the caregiver must be able to swim well. If you commute by train to work, is your childcare starting time set in stone based upon the train schedule or can you always take a later train? Keep in mind that you are seeking high quality, suitable, and reliable childcare. While you now have a good idea of what you need for the first two items, reliability should not be forgotten because without it you may no longer be a *working* parent.

TYPES OF CHILDCARE ARRANGEMENTS

There are several options in choosing a childcare arrangement, although all fall into one of two categories: *in-home* or *out-of-home*. *Out-of-home* childcare has two primary forms: *family day care* and *center-based day care*. Both of these options are provided at a location other than your own home so that you must transport your child (and "supporting equipment" such as diapers or snacks, etc.) to the center. Family day care is provided in someone's home with a caregiver who is usually both a mother and the proprietor (as well as the homeowner). Often she too has young or school-age children and there are usually a small number of children attending a fairly informal program. Center-based day care is found in the more traditional "day-care center" and tends to have a greater number of children enrolled with more structured programs.

In-home childcare is, as it sounds, provided in your home by a caregiver who either lives with you (*live-in*) or who arrives at a scheduled time, usually the start of the workday (*live-out*). In-home caregivers are commonly referred to as nannies, although in my mind there are two types: *au pairs* and *all the others*. A genuine au pair (because some use the term loosely to mean a young nanny) is a young foreigner who is legally in the U.S. on a one-year visa, for the purpose of living and learning about another culture with a family. During that time, the au pair provides childcare for the family in exchange for a small salary, travel and insurance expenses, room and board. The terms of the visa specify some working conditions (only forty-five hours weekly) and often that the au pair must take some educational courses while in the U.S. Au pairs are usually placed through agencies that specialize in this service (see the chapter on search resources for details) and provide some social activities for the au pairs in the area. The rest of the in-home caregiver universe is loosely covered by the term *nanny* (or sometimes simply *baby-sitter*). You will find that some nannies have actually completed courses in childcare and received certification from the educational institution; the majority of nannies, however, are individuals who provide childcare without such formal preparation (although they may have plenty of experience and other training).

As you begin this part of your search, it is important to recognize that not all the childcare arrangements that exist may be available in your area. In our community, we are fortunate that we can choose from all four types; in some parts of the country, this broad selection simply may not be offered or readily available. Make an effort to be open to at least two possible arrangement options on a preliminary basis so that you have some flexibility once you begin to research your options.

The chart on pages 33–36 details the advantages and disadvantages of each basic type of childcare option to help you to identify which type of arrangement best suits your own family's needs.

IN-HOME CHILDCARE

LIVE-IN		LIVE-OUT	
Advantages	Disadvantages	Advantages	Disadvantages
Reliability • Caregiver is always in your home and thus, prompt. Less likelihood for caregiver emergencies. • If your child is ill, childcare is still provided. • Day usually starts and ends according to your own schedule and has some flexibility.	*Reliability* • Backup care in the event of caregiver illness or vacation is not always available. • Legal foreign au pairs can only stay in the job for one year.	*Reliability* • If your child is ill, childcare is still provided. • Day usually starts and ends according to your own schedule and has some flexibility.	*Reliability* • Dependent upon childcare provider's promptness and reliability before you can start the day. • Backup care in the event of caregiver illness or vacation must be prearranged and may not always be available.
Environment • Your child is in a familiar and comfortable setting. • Childcare activities are tailored to meet your child's specific needs and schedule.	*Privacy* • Some loss of family privacy since you have a nonfamily member living in your home. • May be serving as surrogate family for a young nanny or au pair.	*Environment* • Your child is in a familiar and comfortable setting. • Childcare activities are tailored to meet your child's specific needs and schedule.	*Cost* • Can be somewhat costly compared to family and center day care. Usually have to offer other benefits along with salary. • May need to provide car for childcare provider. • Extra expenses of car insurance, food, and utilities.

IN-HOME CHILDCARE (cont'd)

LIVE-IN		LIVE-OUT	
Advantages	Disadvantages	Advantages	Disadvantages
Other: • Caregiver may be willing to help with household errands and chores. • Very convenient. No transporting your child or supplies to another location.	*Cost:* • Can be somewhat costly compared to family and center day care. Usually have to offer other benefits along with salary. • Extra expenses of car insurance, food, and utilities related to having another person in your home.	*Privacy:* • Able to have more family privacy since childcare provider leaves at the end of the day.	*Other:* • Need to deal more directly with personality issues since the childcare provider is in close contact with you as a sole and direct manager.
	Other: • May need to provide car for nanny. • Must have spare living space for nanny. • Need to deal more directly with personality issues since the childcare provider is in direct contact with you as manager.	*Other:* • May be able to get some help with household errands and chores. • Very convenient. Do not have to transport your child or supplies to another location.	

OUT-OF-HOME CHILDCARE

FAMILY DAY CARE		CENTER-BASED DAY CARE	
Advantages	Disadvantages	Advantages	Disadvantages
Reliability: • Childcare provider is always there so that drop-off (or pickup) time is not a problem once negotiated. • If your child is mildly ill, childcare *may* still be provided (depends on your particular arrangement).	*Reliability:* • Backup care in the event of childcare provider illness or vacation is not always available. • Emergency childcare arrangements should be considered in advance.	*Reliability:* • Arrangement is usually very reliable; childcare provider or backup should always be available (unless your child is ill).	*Reliability* • Very limited or no flexibility in scheduling (for example, late pickups are usually fined, etc.) • If your child is ill, usually cannot bring to center (some centers do offer "sick bays").
Environment: • Your child is in a homey comfortable setting with some other children.	*Environment:* • Child's day may be somewhat unstructured and subject to childcare provider's own schedule. • Childcare is not always tailored to meet your child's unique needs and schedule.	*Environment:* • Child's day will be somewhat structured, very child-oriented, with companionship. • Usually features a wide variety of activities and enrichment programs.	*Environment:* • Childcare is not tailored to meet your child's unique needs and schedule. • Your child is in a larger group in a more institutional setting. You also have less control.

OUT-OF-HOME CHILDCARE (cont'd.)

FAMILY DAY CARE		CENTER-BASED DAY CARE	
Advantages	Disadvantages	Advantages	Disadvantages
	Environment: • You must allow the childcare provider more latitude than if it were in your own home.		*Environment:* • May be a lot of childcare provider turnover.
Cost • Usually fairly affordable childcare alternative. May offer multiple-child discount.	*Other:* • Usually provides only childcare support, so help with errands, etc., is not available.	*Cost:* • Usually fairly affordable childcare alternative. May offer multiple-child discount.	*Other:* • Usually provides only childcare support, so help with errands, etc., is not available.
Other: • Often some flexibility in scheduling.	*Other:* • Need to deal more directly with personality issues since the childcare provider is in close contact with you as the manager.	*Other:* • Rules are very clearly spelled out. Conflicts with childcare providers usually have established means of resolution.	

WHAT DOES IT COST AND CAN I AFFORD IT?

Your final choice of a childcare arrangement inevitably must be made against the backdrop of your budget. It is fruitless to select a live-in nanny arrangement when your finances can most realistically support the cost of a quality day-care center. Think carefully about your budget and your financial priorities before you decide what amount you *can* pay versus what you are *willing* to pay. Your childcare goal is to find the best quality that you can afford. This may mean choosing a very high-quality family day care

COST OF CHILDCARE ARRANGEMENTS	
TYPE OF ARRANGEMENT	PRICE RANGE
In-Home: Live-In	From $200 to $500 (or more) weekly depending upon factors such as experience and the number/ ages of children. Add in the hidden cost of room and board plus car and liability insurance, payroll taxes, au pair air fare (if applicable), etc., as applicable to get the true cost.
In-Home: Live-Out	About $150 to $500 (or more) weekly depending upon factors such as experience and the number/ ages of children. Sometimes can be more costly than live-in caregiver, especially because room and board are not provided in the job benefits. Add in the cost of payroll taxes, liability insurance, etc., as applicable.
Out-of-Home: Family Day Care	About $75 to $250 weekly depending upon the age of the child (e.g., infants often cost much more), facility staffing, and amenities.
Out-of-Home: Day-Care Center	About $75 to $250 weekly depending upon the age of the child (e.g., infants often cost much more), facility, staffing, and amenities.

at $225 weekly instead of an inexperienced live-in nanny at $150. The chart on page 37 summarizes the cost ranges for the childcare options discussed earlier (prices will vary depending on where you live).

WHAT! INSURANCE AND TAXES???

Although mentioned in the preceding chart, taxes and insurance require more discussion. While your chief concern in finding quality childcare is to get the most reliable, suitable, and best caregiver and arrangement to meet your family's and child's needs, part of this process also involves your transformation into a manager. With this comes the same type of responsibilities that your own manager has, namely employee relations and management, plus the inevitable: taxes and insurance. These points are sensitive and can be especially thorny if you use in-home or unlicensed out-of-home childcare. (There is a more detailed discussion of taxes and insurance for out-of-home childcare in chapter 8.) At a minimum, you need to be aware that these issues exist, and understand them.

While the situation can vary from one locality to another, and **all readers are directed to their own insurance agents for definitive advice,** it is generally accepted that hiring a caregiver means reviewing your own insurance coverage and perhaps the caregiver's insurance coverage as well.

The bottom line is to consult with your insurance agent regarding coverage of your car and home, and the caregiver while she is your employee.

INSURANCE CONSIDERATIONS

CAR INSURANCE	If the caregiver will be transporting your child while working, then the caregiver is acting as your "agent" and you could be held responsible if something happens. Start by answering the question, whose car is being used? (**Reminder**: You must first confirm that the caregiver has a valid driver's license that will be accepted in your locality. This may be problematic if the caregiver is not a legal resident of the U.S., and also a possible issue if it is an out-of-state or an international driver's license.)
IN YOUR CAR?	It is prudent to explore adding the caregiver to your car insurance as an operator of your car. This should cover certain costs and liability in the event that accident-related expenses are incurred (including being sued and certain medical expenses that might arise from an accident). Even with proper car insurance, many insurance agents also recommend that the parent consider purchasing an umbrella liability policy (see page 40). This is also important to do if the caregiver has off-duty use of your car as a job benefit.
IN HER CAR?	If your child is in a licensed family or day-care center, you should confirm that the vehicles are insured for commercial use (and the drivers are appropriately licensed). For all other types of childcare (in or out of home), at a minimum, the caregiver should have her own valid car insurance with sufficient coverage. Even if the caregiver does have her own valid car insurance, many insurance agents also recommend that the employer consider purchasing an umbrella policy (see page 40).

INSURANCE CONSIDERATIONS (cont'd.)	
UMBRELLA LIABILITY INSURANCE	Whenever someone acts on your behalf (as your agent), there exists the possibility that if something goes wrong, you can be held liable and may be sued or have to pay certain expenses. An umbrella liability policy may provide additional coverage in the event that the liability coverage contained in your homeowner's and car insurance is not sufficient or not applicable to the situation. Ask your agent about available coverage. Umbrella policies tend to be relatively inexpensive for a significant amount of protection, and thus buy a lot of peace of mind.
HOMEOWNER'S POLICY	Check to confirm that your homeowner's policy includes sufficient coverage for personal liability and for damage to your home or other property. The policy also should have some coverage for worker's compensation, although it may be limited to "occasional" workers on your property (such as a repairman hired to fix your dishwasher). If you have regular in-home childcare, which means that a worker (the caregiver) is frequently in your home for lengthy periods of time, then your insurance agent may recommend that you upgrade your existing homeowner's policy with respect to the worker's compensation endorsement.

The issue of taxes is even more complex. **All readers are strongly urged to speak with their own accountants or financial advisors regarding this matter and their specific situation.** The fact is that caregivers should pay taxes on their compensation. The reality is that many caregivers are paid off the books, meaning that the parents do not make requisite deductions or payments for the caregiver's various payroll taxes and that the caregivers do not pay any taxes on their earnings. The reasons for this situation are many but usually start with the fact that many caregivers cannot afford to pay taxes while supporting themselves on their earnings and thus request off-the-books (i.e., cash) compensation, while many parents cannot afford the extra cost related to payroll taxes (which can add 15 percent or more to childcare costs/caregiver's salary) and/or are intimidated by the amount of paperwork and regulation related to these taxes. While the practice of paying off the books is against the law and means that the caregiver is not eligible for the accompanying retirement, disability, or unemployment benefits, it is long-standing and very common for the reasons noted above. The most notable exception to this practice are licensed family and center-based day care.

The following is an overview of *some* of the taxes that an employer of a caregiver may have to withhold or fund (Note: this list can vary according to where you live).

- federal income tax
- state income tax (if applicable)
- city income tax (if applicable)
- Social Security tax
- Medicare
- workers' compensation
- federal unemployment tax
- state unemployment tax

In addition to withholding for these taxes (and in some cases, matching payments on a portion thereof), the parent also must prepare and send periodic tax-related filings (quarterly, semiannually, and annually) along with these payments and provide a W2 form to the caregiver at year-end. There are some accounting firms that specialize in preparing this paperwork specifically for employers of household help. The fees vary, but tend to be a few hundred dollars annually. Depending upon your own resources and aptitude, this expense can be worthwhile given the complex tax and reporting requirements in some parts of the country.

Of note, there are some benefits for the working parent who takes the time and energy to file, withhold, and/or pay all these taxes, namely a possible deduction of a portion of the childcare costs on the parent's income tax returns and a potential "subsidy" on the childcare expenditures through a dependent-care spending account (if offered by the parent's own employer). These accounts allow the parent to save pretax dollars—deducted directly from their paycheck—into special accounts that can be used to reimburse recognized childcare outlays. The use of *pretax* dollars reduces the effective cost of childcare for the parent by the amount of income taxes that is saved—usually at the parent's marginal (and thus highest) tax rate.

There is a ceiling on the amount per child that can be deducted on a parent's income tax (about $2,500 per child) as well as on the amount available through the dependent-care account (this varies from firm to firm, but is usually no more than $5,000 in pretax dollars). Still, the total savings can add up to a few thousand dollars each year, and thus offset some of the costs associated with payroll taxes.

Parents who use childcare at a licensed center that in turn pays the appropriate taxes, or who withhold taxes for in- or out-of-home care should certainly explore possible income tax deductions for childcare expenses and whether their own employer sponsors a dependent-care account to subsidize some of these costs with pretax dollars.

TOUGH COMPROMISES AND CHOICES: YOURS AND OURS

After reviewing the general characteristics of each childcare alternative (including their relative costs), compare these options to your Job Description and select the best and most viable match. Focus on finding the right mix, meaning a *compatible and realistic blend* of the Candidate Qualifications, the Job Requirements, and last, but certainly not least, your budget. To ensure that you are still on target after you have made your preliminary choice, answer the following key questions:

1. Can I afford the compensation for the *type* of arrangement that my needs (Candidate Qualifications and Job Requirements) seem to dictate?
2. Are my budget and compensation on target to attract the *best-qualified* candidate in this arrangement?

If you can answer yes to both of the above questions, you are in the position to start the actual search process. If not, you must go back to your Candidate Qualifications and Job Requirements and begin making compromises that will lead you to the best childcare arrangement that you can afford. Remember, you should not compromise on the most important points, but you may need to give ground on some of your other requirements. It may take time to make some tough choices.

Your guiding principle is to find a loving childcare provider and a safe, reliable arrangement that will make your child feel happy and secure, so you will start by assessing your other requirements for possible flexibility. It is crucial that you remain open-minded during this process. Here are some types of conflicts you may face, and hypothetical compromises:

- If you really want someone to give your child individualized attention and to help with household chores but find that the price to get a quality in-home childcare provider is out of your range, remind yourself that the priority is quality childcare not housekeeping. Consider using quality family day care or a day-care center that also offers some support services (like dry cleaning drop-off) or is located near some service providers. You can continue to do some of the errands yourself or pay someone for three hours a week to do them for you.

- If you had wanted the homelike setting of family day care but none is available in your community, consider in-home care and also visit day-care centers to see if any have an environment that may come close to meeting this requirement.

- If you wanted to hire someone who is specifically trained in childcare (e.g., a nanny program) for an in-home position but that qualification puts the cost over your budget, consider either candidates who lack specific training but have some other childcare experience *or* a family or day-care center with trained caregivers.

- If you had hoped to find a childcare provider near your home but cannot find any that are suitable, explore the childcare options near your office or that of your spouse. Think about whether you would be willing to have your child "commute" with one of you to day care.

- If you really wanted a live-out caregiver but cannot afford one, consider whether you could share the cost and services of one caregiver with another family who lives nearby and alternate in which home the care is provided.

Many times, the candidates for live-in childcare providers do not live in or even near to your community. Unless you are willing to pay for round-trip transportation to your home for a personal face-to-face interview (in the case of foreign au pairs this may be particularly impractical), you will be screening and interviewing only by telephone. That means you may first meet the caregiver in person when she arrives to start working with your child. Determine if you are comfortable with that constraint. Keep this in mind as you select your childcare arrangement.

Rest assured that all parents (including me) experience moments of panic when it appears that the gap between reality and the ideal is too wide to span. Squash any impulse to give up and make a rash decision; instead try to accept the challenge and face the situation squarely. Do your best within the context of your resources and focus your energy on productively making progress in your search.

Once my husband and I got over the hurdle of accepting that we would indeed be hiring a caregiver and making compromises along the way, we were constructively able to take the steps needed to reach our goal. Using the Candidate Qualifications and Job Requirements formulated after Sam was born, we identified his foremost need as being loved and cared for in a comforting, enjoyable, and secure place. To us that meant it would probably be an arrangement in either our home or someone else's. Moreover, since we needed to begin our commute before the opening hours of most area day-care centers, and we preferred not to start later and work later, a day-care center was effectively eliminated from contention. Knowing how much we could afford for compensation/benefits versus the relative costs of live-in, live-out, and family day care, we decided that a family day-care arrangement would be the best fit in terms of getting the highest quality caregiver for our budget.

We then focused on finding the person who fit our Candidate Qualifications, could meet the Job Requirements and offered the most suitable arrangement for our needs (family day care). We were fortunate to find a caregiver who was also the mother of two boys (ages three and six) and who lived in our town. After her oldest was born, she began to care for one or two younger children in her home (family day care), welcoming them into the routine of their daily lives. Sam would go on trips to the market and the park, play with other children, and nap in a bedroom and eat in a kitchen.

Based on the updated Job Requirements we had formulated after Adam turned one year old, we concluded that in-home childcare was our best option given our desire to have some help with chores and to let the boys have a more relaxed morning schedule. Given the early hours and military precision of our morning schedule (because we commuted by train, we could not afford to leave even three minutes late), we further concluded that looking for a live-in nanny would be our first choice (now we also had the space thanks to our recent move to a larger home).

You are now more explicitly aware of the who, what, where, and when of your childcare needs as well as educated on the potential childcare arrangements to consider. With the preparation you have done, your most suitable childcare arrangement will be fairly evident. However, until you have made this determination, restrain yourself from moving ahead.

Identifying Your Search Resources and Starting Your Search

BEFORE YOU CAN begin to find the candidates and arrangements, you must find out *how* to find them. You cannot go to the beach for a ski holiday; you will never find a formal gown in a store that sells hiking outfits. So much energy can be wasted just on figuring out where to look or by looking in the wrong places that parents become exhausted and discouraged before they get to the actual selection process. Your objective is to look in the right places and in the most productive fashion so that you will be directed to the most appropriate selection of caregivers and arrangements for your family. This chapter will help you to identify and select effective search resources and offer advice on how to use them most productively.

Generally speaking, the best way to start identifying search resources is to have a big mouth and to be pleasantly aggressive. Let everyone know that you are looking for childcare. This includes other parents in your community, nannies you see at the park, the pediatrician, co-workers, neighbors, relatives, friends, etc. You will find that there are leads everywhere: the name of good employment agencies, a mother a few blocks away who runs a family day care, a local nanny who is looking for a new position, newspapers that have productive classified ads, etc. You do not have to pursue each of these leads actively, however you should not immediately dismiss any because you never know which one will yield the person/arrangement that you are seeking.

When I started to look for Sam's childcare provider, the entire *universe* knew about it. I used many of the search resources discussed in this chapter: word of mouth, classified ads, employment agencies, community childcare referral agencies, and employer-supported search services. In our case, word of mouth was the key to finding our first caregiver (and an employment agency was the key for the second). After six weeks of discouraging interviews and dead ends, I heard about a family day-care provider through another working mother who was a colleague of my mother (a high school teacher, also with a big mouth, who told everyone *she* worked with about my search). This mother had been using the same family day-care provider to watch her son for two years (since he was an infant); the caregiver would watch no more than two children (plus her own two boys). Most importantly, the second "client" mother was stopping work to be an at-home mom so the caregiver now had an opening. Because my husband and I were prepared, we were ready to act once we found the right person. Indeed, I already knew what sort of person I was looking for, what sort of environment I wanted, and what kind of arrangement would be most suitable. On the face of it, this caregiver seemed to fit our needs. I called her up, introduced myself, screened her by phone, and arranged to visit her home for a face-to-face interview. We met, the situation and personal dynamics addressed all our parameters, and the rest is history.

After four years with the same family day-care provider,

we reevaluated our needs and Job Requirements and began a new search for a live-in nanny. This search required even more time and energy because our Job Requirements were more complex. Again, we let the world know that we were looking for childcare although nanny employment agencies were our most effective search tool. Even though we were well prepared, this search took us *six months* of interviewing, all the while reassessing whether our expectations and fundamental requirements were set so high that we would never find someone (and deciding each time that we should stick to our guns to get the quality of caregiver that we knew our children deserved). We found that there was a lot of competition from other families for high quality in-home caregivers. At times, the search became very disheartening and we sometimes took short breaks of a few days to reenergize. After each round of applications, interviews, and references, I gave feedback to the agencies and recruiters with whom we were working so that they would be equipped to recognize the right person when she came along. Finally we interviewed a prospective nanny and found that we got along, our children liked her, and she had excellent references. We offered her the job. It was not an easy search but it resulted in our finding a wonderful live-in nanny who was with us for three years.

HOW LONG DOES THIS TAKE?

The search will take a lot of your time and energy—inevitably more than you anticipate—so be prepared. The exact length of time that the childcare search requires is variable. Generally, you should allow yourself at least two to three months for the search, especially if you have advance notice of your need for childcare (i.e., you know when your maternity leave is ending or when your current childcare arrangement will be terminating). This does not include the week or two that your preparation process requires. If luck is on your side, your search might take as little as a week once you are in the position to commence. However, it could take six months (as it did for us with our live-in nanny), six weeks (as it did for us with the family day-care provider), or anything in between.

If you are interested in using out-of-home childcare, you may encounter *waiting lists* at some of the better-quality programs and centers. When doing your preliminary search for resources, you should make an effort to determine if this is an issue with any of the centers in your pool of choices. If so, try accelerating your lead time so that you can interview and visit sites (see the next chapter) and get your name on the waiting list to give yourself time to move up to the top. You may also have to consider an interim childcare arrangement until you are able to enroll your child in the center that is your first choice.

LOOKING IN THE RIGHT PLACES: IDENTIFYING AND ENLISTING SEARCH RESOURCES TO HELP YOU FIND CHILDCARE

There are a variety of resources and tools to help you in your search for quality childcare. The trick is understanding what they are and how they can help you. Here are some ways in which you can begin to identify these resources:

- Word of mouth is an often underestimated resource. Ask your pediatrician, clergyman, neighbors, co-workers, and other parents to recommend the agencies, day-care providers, and community services that may be in your area. Unless people know that you are in the market for quality childcare, you will not get this information. I found two excellent childcare employment agencies through conversations with our pediatrician and with a colleague at my office.

- Look in the Yellow Pages under Child Care, Day-Care Centers, and anything else you can think of that might be vaguely related.
- Call your local assemblyman, state senator, county free-holder, mayor, or councilman to ask if there are any community childcare referral services or any other programs for working families that could help you.
- Read the local newspapers, including regular and classified ads. Look under headings such as Child-Care Services, Services Offered, Employment Wanted, Household Help Wanted, Employment Agencies.
- Check out ethnic newspapers that may be published in your area, since newer immigrants and citizens are often interested in childcare positions. (For example, in my area, the *Irish Echo* contains numerous ads for childcare agencies, situations wanted, and employment offered, and thus provides valuable leads.)
- Ask at local college employment offices if they have a career placement service or if they have a childcare certification program through which you could recruit.
- Use the Internet or visit your local library for books on childcare and lists of clubs or societies that focus on childcare—e.g., a chapter of the International Nanny Association (INA), the National Association for the Education of Young Children (NAEYC), etc.—or "nanny schools" (there are several in the U.S.). Appendix H (page 201) contains several national resources that offer some guidance and support.
- Ask your supervisor and human resources department if your employer offers a childcare referral or support program. If you are especially lucky, you may have an employer who actually offers an on-site childcare center (be aware that there may be a long waiting list).

As you get feedback from these inquiries, be sure that you write down the ideas and suggestions you may hear. This includes names of agencies or providers (both good and bad), ideas on Candidate Qualifications and Job Requirements, interviewing suggestions and "dos and don'ts" extracted from the experiences of others. Even if a contact does not yield a strong search lead, ask the contact person if he or she has any other ideas or contacts to recommend to you. Follow up on all leads and suggestions until you are able to identify those that will be most productive for you in your search. The following is an overview of which resource is usually most productive for specific childcare options:

CHILDCARE SEARCH RESOURCES	
RESOURCE	BEST IF YOU ARE LOOKING FOR:
Community Referral Agency and Employer Referral Service	Referral services are usually flexible in how they can help you. They will ask what type of arrangement you are looking for and provide you with search resources accordingly. For example, if you want day-care centers, they might provide you with a list of those in your area; for in-home care, a list of local employment agencies, etc. They might also have materials that provide helpful hints on choosing childcare.
Au pair Placement Agency	Au pairs are foreigners (usually young women) who come to the U.S. on one-year J-1 visas. The placement agencies recruit and screen these applicants through overseas offices. The au pair may legally work up to 45 hours weekly and also need to take some type of classes to qualify for their visas (classes are broadly defined and could include programs at the YMCA or night school).

CHILDCARE SEARCH RESOURCES (cont'd.)

RESOURCE	BEST IF YOU ARE LOOKING FOR:
Nanny Schools	There are several educational programs that train students for childcare positions, some of which are accredited by the NAEYC or INA. Some programs are oriented toward in-home (specifically live-in) childcare while others also train providers for center-based programs. The quality of these programs varies but all share the common feature of a concentrated pool of candidates interested in childcare positions. Many of these programs offer placement services through related fee-based employment agencies (see below); others permit you to post your position directly at no cost. (See Appendix C for sample letters for posting your job.)
Classified Ads	Best for finding in-home care (live-in or live out) and sometimes for locating family day care.
Childcare Consultants	Consultants (which are not very common) help you to have a productive search by ascertaining which of the search resources are most likely to yield candidates to meet your needs. They may also offer interview screening, reference checking, and related services.
Childcare Employment Agency	Employment agencies usually recruit providers of in-home childcare; some may be connected to a nanny school. Some agencies recruit young women from other parts of the country while others tend to have immigrants or local candidates on their rosters. In our area, there is also an agency that specializes in placing children in licensed family day care, and also supervises these providers with regular on-site visits as well as offering continuing training to them.

Once you have identified the resources best suited to helping you find the type of childcare you desire, you can begin to use them to locate qualified candidates. For example, if you already have targeted day-care centers as the best childcare arrangement to meet your family's needs, then placing classified ads and using employment agencies (both of which will produce either in-home or family day-care candidates) will not suit your search. Instead, you may find that community or employer referral services, word of mouth, the Yellow Pages and newspaper ads (placed by day-care centers) will be more helpful. Alternatively, if you decide to use an employment agency, make sure you select one that is reputable and has a solid track record—no need to be someone's practice client. Later in this chapter (page 62), there is extensive advice on how to choose a quality childcare employment agency. Be willing to use a variety of search resources but be selective in which ones you specifically choose by focusing on those that will be the most productive for your particular needs.

PREPARING YOUR "MARKETING PACKAGE"

A key component to a successful search is getting people interested in the opportunity to work with your child by effectively communicating your needs to both search resources and prospective candidates. For in-home care candidates especially, this information can be very effectively communicated in the form of a Marketing Package. (The marketing package is usually not needed in the search for out-of-home childcare.) The Candidate Qualifications and Job Requirements you created, besides shaping your search, are important tools that you can use to attract quality candidates. One invariable fact in finding quality childcare is that demand far exceeds supply; you need to think in terms of "selling" potential candidates on your childcare position so that they become interested in "selling" you on their qualifications to fill it. You are trying to differentiate your position from all the other childcare positions from which the caregiver can choose. *The competition for the best caregivers is intense. Never assume that everyone is already dying to work for you—be prepared to make a compelling presentation.*

You can enhance your marketing package with a description of your children, family life, home, community, etc. In our package, we briefly discussed some of our general parenting and family philosophies. If you are comfortable with the concept, you may even want to include a photo of your children and home as we did. Pictures of your children can be especially appealing to the caregiver who truly loves kids (who ever saw a "not cute" child?). Make your marketing package as attractive (but realistic) as possible (do not omit any important Candidate Qualifications or Job Requirements). You cannot hire the perfect caregiver if they never apply, and your objective is to get as many qualified candidates as possible to apply. There is no such thing as too many applicants; you can quickly eliminate those who are unqualified. The following is the marketing package we used in our search for live-in help.

NANNY POSITION

Employer: Michelle Ehrich and Andrew Ross
Address and Phone

Children: Sam Ross (born July 1990)
Adam Ross (born January 1993)

Family Description: (Note to the reader: This is a big part of our "selling" the job.)

The primary focus in our lives is our family. When we have free time, we seek to spend it with the children, usually just hanging out and playing. It is very important to us that we try to have a family dinner every night (however simple the meal) and that we put the kids to bed with a bath and story. Since we do spend a large part of our day at work, we want to ensure that our free time is well spent and, to us, that means with our kids.

Sam is a very good-natured and bright preschooler. He has a good vocabulary and excellent reasoning skills. In addition, he is quite tall and physically dexterous for his age. He is also very shy around strangers and in new situations (even if he knows everyone there), especially if his mom or dad is around to keep him company. In that respect, we've been told he takes after both his parents as children.

Adam is a very happy and laid-back toddler with a sweet disposition. He goes with the flow although he does love to sit on our laps and is a real climber. He has also demonstrated more of a mischievous streak than his brother had at the same age. The boys get along well and are starting to play together nicely although there is still some sibling rivalry to overcome.

Michelle grew up in a small town in New Jersey and Andrew comes from a small town in Upstate New York. We both work in Manhattan at banks.

Our family is Jewish and we observe the major religious holidays. We are not Orthodox in our beliefs, which means that we do not go to temple every week, nor do we follow a special diet. We have a wide range of friends of all religions.

Position Description: (Note to the reader: This is taken directly from our Job Description.)
1. Primary responsibility: The children are your first and most important responsibility, everything else (e.g., laundry, dishes, etc.) is secondary. They need to be played with, read to, cared for while we are at work. We are looking for someone who will actively interact with our

children and not just watch them. We hope that you will be a positive role model for our children, teaching them kindness, confidence, responsibility, and consideration.

2. General duties revolve around caring for our children while we are at work:

- Get children up and dressed in the morning; bathe them before we get home for dinner.
- Prepare children's breakfast and lunch and start family dinner; clean up kitchen after breakfast and lunch. On infrequent occasions when we have an evening engagement, you may be asked to prepare the children's dinner and clean up.
- Keep children's bedrooms and playroom neat. Do children's laundry, mending, etc.
- Drive children to preschool and other daytime activities and appointments (pediatrician, etc.).
- Entertain children during the day with activities at home and in the yard, and with trips to park, library, shops in town, etc.
- Do a limited amount of local errands with children if time permits (including the grocery shopping with Adam when Sam is in school).

3. Days and hours: We usually leave for work by 6:20 A.M. and return by 6:00 P.M. You are on duty when we are out of the house, even if the children are still asleep. You will be working from Monday morning through Friday evening with weekday evenings free. You will be off from Friday evening until Monday morning.

4. Tenure: We are seeking someone who, upon finding an enjoyable childcare position, is interested in staying for at least eighteen to twenty-four months.

Candidate Qualifications: (Note to the reader: This is taken directly from our Candidate Qualifications.)

- Genuine love and appreciation of children and desire to care for them.

- Prior childcare experience. Childcare training (e.g., nanny certificate) is a welcome credential.
- Good judgment and common sense.
- Energetic and enjoys playing with children.
- Well spoken.
- Creative.
- No smoking. No drug use or alcohol abuse, past or present.
- Good health and grooming.
- Three work references (at least two childcare); two personal references (nonfamily); family references (we will want to speak with your parents and/or children).
- Clean driving record (and valid driver's license) and no police record. Experience in heavy suburban driving is a plus.
- High school graduate and some college or nanny courses.
- Some first aid knowledge.
- Basic cooking skills.
- Lived away from home for at least three months.

(Note to the reader: The next two sections comprise the compensation and benefits that we considered when we formulated the job description/requirements.)

Amenities and Accommodations:

Private bedroom: New bed and furniture, TV, clock radio, phone with separate line and answering machine. You are responsible for all toll calls on this line.

Shared bathroom with the children: This is a very large and renovated hall bathroom, which also houses the washer and dryer. There is plenty of cabinet space for storage of personal items. Since the children are so young, with the exception of bath time in the evenings, they spend little time using this room.

Playroom/den: We have a large, newly finished playroom, which is carpeted and furnished. When the toys are put away, it serves as a den. You may use this room to entertain friends when you are off duty provided the children are not using it.

Car: We have two cars. During the week, one will be available to you to transport the children or if you go out at night. On the weekend, you may have personal use of the car *most of the time and with our agreement.* You are expected to drive carefully and to pay for any damage you may cause to the car or tickets you receive.

Compensation:
Salary: To be determined. A raise will be considered annually.
Vacation: Two weeks (ten working days) plus two days at Christmas. If you are asked to accompany us on vacation to work, compensation will be prearranged. We do ask that you coordinate your vacation plans with ours. In addition, we recommend (although it is certainly not a requirement) that you plan to take some extra time off around the Christmas holiday.
Holidays: There are a total of six holidays—New Year's Day, President's Day, Memorial Day, July 4th, Thanksgiving Day, and Christmas Day.

Community and Neighborhood: (Note to the reader: This is a big part of our "selling" the job.)

Westfield is truly a lovely town with a great sense of civic pride. The town, located in the suburban New York City area, has a population of about thirty thousand and is two hundred years old. Most of the streets are tree lined and there is a mix of Victorian, colonial, and newer homes. Among the activities in town are a local symphony, a community theater and orchestra, a community pool, YMCA, an arts workshop and recreation programs, various recreational clubs, several churches of virtually all denominations, several town parks with playgrounds, lakes, tennis, soccer, baseball, and basketball facilities, and a newly expanded public library. Westfield is well known for an excellent school system that also offers a wonderful adult school with night classes on a tremendous variety of subjects. There is also a large downtown with two movie theaters (five screens), dozens of restaurants (Chinese, Italian, French, Japanese, American, etc.), over a hundred shops, and a large upscale department store. Westfield has train and bus lines into New York City; it is about a forty-five minute ride and many residents commute to jobs in New York or go in to enjoy the cultural attractions there. In addition, the town is about thirty miles from the Jersey beaches on the Atlantic, among the nicest in the Northeast.

Our neighborhood is unique in that it is a quiet area yet just a short walk to downtown, the train, and the bus. The homes are older and well maintained. Our neighbors are very friendly (there is a summer block party and a holiday party in the winter) and there are lots of kids.

(Note to the reader: We included photos of both boys and of our home.)

THE COST OF HIRING HELP FOR YOUR SEARCH

The search for quality childcare tends to cost money unless you are fortunate enough to find a caregiver by word of mouth. The following is a schedule of the average prices for the various search resources:

CHILDCARE SEARCH RESOURCES— AVERAGE PRICE RANGES

Resource	Average Price Range
Community Referral Agency and Employer Referral Service	Usually free or sliding scale fee, but may refer you to childcare employment agencies or other resources that charge a fee.
Nanny Schools	If the school permits you to post your position or contact candidates directly, then there is usually no cost. If not, the fees are comparable to an employment agency (see below).
Childcare Consultants	These services offer advice on your search, do candidate or reference screening, etc. Consultants often charge by the hour ($25–$75) or by the specific service. If they work efficiently, it may cost less than an agency.
Childcare Employment Agency	Usually charge a registration fee ($50–$150) plus a placement fee that ranges from two or three weeks' salary to $1,300–$2,000 flat. Sometimes comes with limited "replacement" guarantee. Also add in your phone charges for interviewing and checking references on long-distance candidates (about $50 or more). Usually you will also pay transportation costs if you hire a long-distance candidate (not counting transportation costs if you want a face-to-face interview before hiring).
Classified Ads	The cost of the ad. In my area, an ad in a widely circulated paper usually costs about $50–$75 a week (for one weekday and Sunday) and in a community paper about $35–$50 a week.

	CHILDCARE SEARCH RESOURCES—(cont'd) AVERAGE PRICE RANGES
Resource	Average Price Range
Au Pair Placement Agency	Usually charge an application fee ($200 or so). If you hire an au pair, you must pay a placement fee, which includes a replacement guarantee, au pair health insurance, and the person's round-trip air transportation from their home country (total is about $4,000). Also add in your international phone charges for interviewing and checking references (about $50 or more). This high fee is offset by a much lower salary you pay an au pair caregiver.

HOW TO SELECT AND EFFECTIVELY USE AN AGENCY OR CONSULTANT

Your preliminary research may uncover employment agencies (or consultants, which I collectively include in this section) that specialize in placing childcare providers in your target arrangement. While these agencies are usually for in-home care (live-in or live-out), there are also some that offer placements in family day-care programs. Generally speaking, if you decide to use an agency, it is a good idea to work with more than one since they will tend to have different applicant pools.

Because you only want to work with agencies or consultants that can produce results for you, check on each one very carefully before you pay any fees or fill out any forms. Here are some very important questions to ask, and the nature of the answers you can reasonably expect to receive.

1. *How do you recruit applicants and what is your screening process?*

Find out their recruiting techniques (ads, marketing trips, etc.)—ask if they concentrate on young women who reside out of your area, local candidates, etc. Review the caregiver application form—if you are not permitted to do so before you pay the registration fee, do not use the agency. Does it ask for only basic information (name, health condition, experience, references, etc.) or does it ask more thoughtful questions (e.g., "Why do want to work as a childcare provider?"; "What do you find most challenging about children?"; "What do you think is the most effective way to discipline a child and why?"; etc.). Find out if the agency actually interviews candidates who have completed the application (in person or by phone?) and of what the interview consists. Ask if they have rejected any candidates and why, as well as what might disqualify a candidate from consideration. Confirm whether and how the agency checks references; make sure that it also checks police, credit, and driving records. Find out what else it may do to screen candidates. The agency should be very thorough in screening before it considers accepting a candidate to place—both in terms of checking records and references as well as in finding out what the candidate is like as a human being.

2. *What information do you require from potential employers?*

You want to work with an agency that makes an effort to match qualified candidates to your particular situation. The employer application form that you will complete ought to be extremely detailed (if an agency will not let you see this before you pay the registration fee, do not even consider using it). It should cover specific and descriptive questions about your family, the job description (including benefits), candidate qualifications, as well as some general ones such as parenting and discipline philosophy, etc. Some may even request that *you* provide personal references so that candidates can get comfortable with your family, etc. (Providing references should not offend you. This shows a professional respect for the candidates and their need to assess a situation fully before accepting an employment offer.)

3. *Do you specialize in any type of candidate or childcare situation? What have you had the most success in?*

Try to use an agency that has had success in placing candidates with families like yours and in jobs like yours. Some agencies only have candidates who will work under certain conditions or are from certain backgrounds. For example, I know of one nanny placement agency that will only consider nanny positions for families that also employ other household help (e.g., housekeeper, gardener, etc.) and for jobs that require only childcare responsibilities (e.g., no family grocery shopping or laundry, etc.). If you had envisioned hiring a childcare provider who would also help out with local errands, this would not be an appropriate agency for you to use. Other agencies recruit most candidates long distance so it may be costly to conduct an in-person interview.

4. *How do you match up candidates and employers?*

Some agencies work very hard to find candidates who meet your specific qualifications before passing the application on to you; others will show you all the "live" candidates to let you decide. Also, some agencies show the job requirements and family write-up to the candidate to assess interest before passing the application on to you; others do not. Use an agency that does this preliminary screening so that you will not waste your time reviewing candidates who do not fit your qualifications or may not be interested in your job.

5. *What support services do you offer to the employers and employees after you have completed a placement?*

Postplacement support services are something that many of the more reputable agencies offer, especially with live-in childcare providers. These services consist of mediating adjustment problems, sponsoring a social group or support network of other local nannies to ease loneliness, etc.

6. *What is your guarantee and replacement policy? Under what conditions, if any, do you give a refund?*

While all families hope that the childcare provider they hire will be a perfect fit and have a long tenure, the sad fact is that things do not always work out. In such cases, the agency that provided the candidate should find a replacement. A replacement policy notes that if the replacement nanny is needed within a few weeks of the first start date, then it will be at no further cost; if it is after that time period but within three to six months (this window can vary by agency), it is at a reduced or prorated fee. Replacement policies often specify that they are applicable only if your job requirements have not changed (in other words, you must be very direct in all your job requirements). Refund policies are much less common (although desirable if you can find it). If an agency does not offer a guarantee and replacement policy or it has one that is unreasonable (only for the first month or less), consider using a different agency.

7. *What are your fees?*

Find out how much the *registration fee* is; whether it applies toward the *placement fee*; how much the placement fee is and the timetable for paying the placement fee. Beware of excessively high registration fees (compared to other agencies in your area) unless that particular agency is especially well recommended as successful because it may not be the one to locate your childcare provider and you will not have anything to show for paying out that hard-earned money. The same goes for the placement fee unless the agency is known to be notably successful in completing searches and offers a very strong replacement policy. In our area, agencies usually charge $50–$200 registration fees; placement fees vary from two or three weeks of the provider's salary or a flat rate of $1,000–$2,000. When we hired a live-in nanny, the agency who found her received a $150 registration fee plus an additional $1,200 placement fee.

The firm came very highly recommended by someone who had used it for eleven years, and also offered a very fair replacement and refund policy.

8. *How long have you been in business?*

Always try to use an agency that is well established and experienced since this is a business that can attract some fly-by-night operators. First, because you are paying fees, you want to ensure that you will get some productive effort in return. Also, well-established agencies tend to attract a larger pool of candidates who also may be more qualified. The only exception is a new agency founded by someone who is very experienced in this field and which charges nominal or no fees up front, reasonable placement fees, and/or offers a refund if a placement cannot be replaced under a guarantee.

9. *To what professional organizations do you or your agency belong?*

If possible (although this is not an absolute requirement), try to use an agency that is a member of a well-known organization in the field of childcare such as the International Nannies Association or the National Association for the Education of Young Children (NAEYC). This shows a commitment to the field and a level of legitimacy.

10. *Please provide three client references, specifically families with whom you have recently placed a caregiver (including at least one repeat customer).*

A reputable agency will proudly provide you with the names and phone numbers of three recent satisfied customers (ask for at least one repeat customer, or better yet, a family who had to use the replacement guarantee). Once you get these references, **follow up with each one.** Ask the following questions:

- What were your needs when you used the agency?
- What services did the agency perform for you? Were your expectations met? Is there any area in which the agency

fell short? If so, what was it and how important was it to you?

- Did you feel that you received personalized treatment in filling your position or that your family was just one of many who were "on the hunt"?

- How would you characterize the quality of the services provided (screening, interviewing, applicant flow, etc.) and, separately, of the candidates you reviewed? How long did it take until you found your childcare provider?

- How many candidates did you see through this agency? Were you satisfied with this flow?

- What type of follow-up support was provided to you and the childcare provider? How do you feel about this coverage?

- If you did use the replacement policy, what kind of treatment/priority did your job get? Were you satisfied with the process and results?

- Do you feel that the fees were reasonable for the services provided?

- Would you use this agency again if you needed to fill another childcare position? Why or why not? (Note: This is my favorite type of question when getting a reference. Human nature is such that people rarely want to say something negative when giving a reference but if asked whether they would use a service again, they tend to answer very thoughtfully and truthfully. You can get a lot of information from the answer to this question.)

When you have chosen the specific agencies or consultants, provide them with your marketing package as well as completed application forms or questionnaires. Make sure that the contact person has a clear understanding of your childcare position and requirements. Request that your marketing package be provided to any candidate who passes the preliminary screening done by the agency (unless the application is extremely thorough, it will not convey the same amount of information as your package, and if it is thorough, it will probably duplicate the information you have already composed in the package so you need not repeat it).

Make an effort to speak with your contact person at the agency on a regular basis; every week or two is ideal. You are paying the agency for its services, meaning that it should be working for you 100 percent of the time; however, the fact is that yours is one of *many* families for which it is trying to find a childcare provider. By regularly communicating with the agency, you are more likely to hear about new applicants as they come in and to have first shot at some of the better-qualified candidates.

In addition to these regular calls, you should provide prompt feedback on all candidates that the agency refers to you for consideration. If you are not interested in setting up an interview, let the agency know why; if you have had an interview, let the agency know what you do and do not like about the candidate and if you do or do not wish to continue interviewing the person and why. This type of feedback helps a good agency to refine its focus in referring candidates to you. The agency will also serve as an interface with the candidates, sparing you the need to tell someone you are not interested or boosting a candidate's ego by telling of your positive impressions.

USING THE NEWSPAPERS MOST EFFECTIVELY

Make a point of looking at the local newspapers during your childcare search (before you start is even better). You may see articles about a new day-care center or a special program at one in your area. You will definitely see advertisements (both regular and classified) offering childcare services (center based, employment agencies—including au pairs, etc.). All these can provide you with resources to find quality childcare. You can also use the newspaper as a place to advertise for an in-home or a family caregiver.

Using the newspaper classified ads can be a very cost-effective way of attracting a large pool of candidates. The downside is that you must do all the screening on your own, possibly taking a lot of phone calls, etc., from people that you might not want to sit near on the bus, let alone permit to watch your children. (Look on page 77 in the chapter titled "Screening and Interviewing," for advice.) With this caveat in mind, I recommend that you do consider using the classifieds as part of your search (for either in-home or family day care), especially if you do not intend to use an employment agency (or even if you do, since the potential savings on the placement fee can be significant).

The first thing you need to do is to write an effective ad, conveying everything of importance contained in your Marketing Package in about four tiny lines or twenty-five words—including your phone number. Not easy! Study the classified ads for childcare in the newspaper for ideas on how to do this. When you call to place your ad, ask about effective ways to abbreviate words as well as what days are the best for placing these types of ads. (For a weekly paper, there is no choice, but for a daily you may want to run it just on weekends or one weekday and Sunday.)

View this exercise like one of those contests you see in the supermarket ("Win a trip to Hawaii—tell us why you love pineapples in fifteen words or less!"); try to pare your presentation down to the bare essentials:

- Basic personality attributes
- Minimum must-have skills
- Basic responsibilities
- Child(ren)'s age(s)
- Hours
- Where (your home or theirs)

- Benefits
- Your phone number

The ad we placed under the Childcare Wanted heading when we were seeking our first childcare provider read as follows:

Cheerful, loving, exp'd person for our infant son; non-smkr, our home or yours; M–F, 6:30 A.M.–5:30 P.M.; refs, compet sal; call 908–555–1212.

When we were looking for our second childcare provider, we placed two ads in different papers:

Energ, caring, exp'd nanny live-in, 2 boys, 4 & 1½. 6:30 A.M.–6 P.M. Clean driv lic, non-smkr, chkble refs req'd. Compet sal & bene. 908–555–1212.

Caring, energ, exp'd nanny to live-in Wstfld for 2 boys, 4 & 1½. 6:30 A.M.–6 P.M. Clean driv lic, non-smkr & chkble refs req. Compet sal & bene. 908–555–1212.

None of these ads were literary masterpieces, yet they did communicate our major requirements. However, there was no separation of the wheat from the chaff in the innumerable responses we received. We spent a lot of time screening for genuinely qualified applicants. Even though we did not find our caregiver through the newspaper, this process helped us to refine our sense of what sort of person we were looking for and gave us the chance to hone our interviewing skills. (We also were able to alert a close friend whose newly hired nanny answered our ad!) We knew many families who did have luck using the paper—it just was not our turn.

As mentioned earlier in this chapter, when identifying

search resources, try to determine which newspapers carry a lot of Childcare Wanted and related advertisements. This usually implies a symbiotic relationship—childcare providers look here so families advertise here. In our area, there is a local weekly paper that covers community events in our county (e.g., the Rescue Squad fund-raiser, the new bookstore in the next town, etc.); it also carries tons of local classified ads for everything from garage sales to lawn services. There are also at least twenty ads each week for childcare providers wanted (and several for positions sought, too). We advertised in this paper both times and had numerous responses. There is also a daily newspaper that covers the half of our state; it has a wide circulation and a big Sunday edition. We advertised in the Sunday paper when we were trying to fill our second position. While the number of responses was not quite as high as in the local weekly paper, we were able to attract even more applicants for consideration.

Our lack of success in finding childcare through the classifieds should not discourage you, especially if you do come across other families who have had positive experiences. The financial investment to use this resource is low and, at a minimum, you will learn some screening and interviewing techniques and perhaps further clarify your childcare qualifications and requirements.

PART II

Action

CHAPTER 6

Screening and Interviewing

YOU ARE NOW at the turning point. Until now, we have focused on developing the means to conduct an effective search for quality childcare and our efforts have been fairly self-contained. This chapter will offer you advice on the process of *screening* and *interviewing* a pool of applicants. The preparation you have undertaken thus far got you started in a productive search; you must now move on to the task of passing judgment on the prospective childcare providers (and/or day-care centers, etc.) that you have found. I will also cover some suggestions on the subtle matter of how to sell your job to a candidate and the importance of making sure that you do so.

What is the difference between screening and interviewing? The goal of *screening* is to make a quick and preliminary determination as to whether the day-care center or the job applicant warrants your further consideration. It is a very brief process (not longer than fifteen minutes or so) that determines if a candidate/center meets the most important factual elements of your requirements, such as prior experience or center hours open.

Interviewing is much more in-depth and focuses upon whether the candidate has the temperament and overall ability to care for your children or if you are comfortable with the caliber of the family or day-care center. I advocate using two types of interviews: by telephone and then face-to-face.

Neither screening nor interviewing is an easy undertaking; both take a lot of time and energy and can sometimes be quite disheartening. Be prepared to screen and interview lots of candidates and then to check the references on the most promising of them. Always have your list of questions ready along with a notepad and pen so that you can record responses and overall impressions. If the going gets really tough, keep a positive attitude and remind yourself:

I will look at many but I only need to find one.

When looking for our first childcare provider, I seriously considered three family and day-care centers—not counting all the people who answered my classified ad and were initially screened by phone. When searching for our live-in nanny, my husband and I read applications from over *fifty* candidates, interviewed at least ten by phone, and hosted four in our home for face-to-face interviews.

Conduct an interview with any caregiver who will be involved with your child, regardless of whether it is in your home or at a family or day-care center. If you plan on using a out-of-home arrangement (family or day-care center), recognize before you start that the center and the caregivers come as a package deal. If you like the caregiver but not the center itself (or visa versa), you cannot take just that which impressed you and leave the other. The center/facility must meet your expectations and the caregivers must meet your Candidate Qualifications. Arrange to interview the director of the program, the relevant childcare "teacher" and, if possible, the aides. In addition to the advice in this chapter, you will find more detailed suggestions regarding center-based interviewing also contained in chapter 8 on on-site visits (page 111).

SCREENING

Although the screening process is not particularly detailed, it will help you to determine if it is worthwhile to spend more time speaking with a candidate and/or center. Remember to refer to your list of questions and to take notes during this process. Screening questions usually cover topics such as childcare experience, availability to satisfy job hours and days, and other basic points. While first impressions are not always correct, you should listen to your gut feelings if something tells you that this is or is not the right candidate or center to consider for your position. If you like what you are hearing, ask the candidate if she is interested in learning more about the position and speaking with your family. If you get a yes in response, you can either begin or schedule a more in-depth interview. Although it is fairly rare, don't feel bad if you hear a no. Just as you might not click with an applicant, the feeling can also go the other way. Be philosophical and recognize that it is better to find out that a candidate is not interested before you hire her rather than after.

On the other hand, if you do not like what you have heard or are the least bit uncomfortable, gracefully end the conversation. For instance, "Thank you for speaking with me. I appreciate your time. Right now I am speaking with several people who are also very qualified, and deciding who we will be seeing for interviews next week. I will call you then if we will be speaking further." Identify what it was that caused you to screen out the candidate—this will help to refine your ability to make a final choice by giving you feedback on reality versus your Candidate Qualifications, Job Requirements, and search methods. Then take a deep breath, keep a positive attitude, and move on to the next candidate.

Screening Individual Candidates (and Dealing with Competition in the Marketplace)

There are two types of individual candidates for childcare that you may be screening: *prequalified candidates*, such as those who are highly recommended or have been screened and referred by an agency (if the agency has not done a thorough screening to prequalify, do not use that agency—see chapter 5 on identifying search resources); and *fresh candidates*, who are usually answering your classified ad. When dealing with a fresh candidate who does not know more about the job than what she has read in an ad, you should convey some more important details of the Job Requirements or Candidate Qualifications. For example, I always asked about previous childcare experience because the lack of this would immediately eliminate a candidate from my consideration. I also always emphasized the starting time (6:30 A.M.), even though it was in the ad, because that was a requirement that some candidates would never consider.

With a prequalified candidate, inquire, "What is it about our position that interests you?" and if applicable, "What is it about your current job that you enjoy and that you dislike?" Ideally, she will say something like she enjoys being with children but dislikes changing forty diapers a day (can you blame her?). In the case of in-home childcare, the candidate may respond that she has read your marketing package and was really attracted to the description of your family, especially the children (I actually did get that answer often), or that the job just sounds like an appealing childcare position with the types of responsibilities and activities that she would find enjoyable or challenging.

When screening a fresh candidate, the first questions to ask are (don't forget to take notes):

• What can I tell you about this position?
• Why are you interested in applying for this position?
• What are you looking for in a position?

The responses to these very basic questions can be very revealing. Your opening question will give you an idea if the candidate is truly interested in a childcare position, or in just getting a job, based upon the type of inquiry you hear in response. (Compare "Tell me about your children and their activities?" to "How much are you paying?") The answer to "Why are you interested in this position?" ought to be along the lines of "I really love to work with children," or "This is the type of work that I enjoy and I am good at." But don't be surprised if you hear something like "Well, I really need the job/the money," or "My lease is expiring so I need a live-in job." (I have gotten both of those replies.) The answer to "What are you looking for in a position?" should reflect sentiments like "A real role in helping to raise a child, assist a family, etc." or "The respect of the family I work for in doing a good job for them." Instead, you may hear "A few days paid vacation and maybe paid sick days if I feel under the weather," or "More money." (I got these answers too.)

After you have finished this very preliminary screening, you will know if the candidate has some of the very basic qualifications you are seeking, i.e., prior experience, hours willing to work, etc. Essentially, you want to ascertain if the applicant is truly interested in working with your children and family, and then, if they meet some of your fundamental requirements. It is fine that the candidate may be attracted to your job by its location, hours, or compensation, but that should not be their primary stated reason for applying. If you are comfortable with the answers you have received in your screening, you are poised to commence a more lengthy initial interview.

Pause at this step in the process if you are considering in-home childcare. I strongly recommend that you take some time now to give the candidate a more detailed description of your children, family, and position *before* you start to ask the more detailed questions in an initial interview. Your goal is to make your family and position stand out and to form a personal connection with the candidate. This dialogue builds up the "selling" that you hope your marketing package has already done. Your shameless objective is to make the strong applicants like you and your family so that they *want* to work with your children and family. *I learned the hard way that if you want to have the luxury of choosing a quality childcare provider, first you must get the best candidates interested in your position and to like you enough to really want the job.*

When I first began to screen and interview live-in nanny candidates by telephone, I spent the bulk of the initial interview (immediately after the screening) discussing Candidate Qualifications and Job Requirements in a very factual and businesslike (yet not unfriendly) manner. In two early instances, once when I called a candidate back for the second interview and once when I spoke to the agency for feedback, I learned that the candidates had since made plans to visit another family (i.e., a face-to-face interview) because they "just hit it off right away with the mother/family" (i.e., employer). *Then it dawned on me: even though I thought that our position and children were the best in the world, there was a lot of competition out there!* Read that sentence again to make sure you remember it!

This was an important lesson. I modified my interviewing methods, adopting a more conversational approach to form a personal connection with the candidate. I began to spend more time initially talking about the personalities of our children, our priorities in life, our perspectives on childcare, and our community, etc., then gradually shifting focus to learning more about the candidate's qualifications. It took a bit more time up front, but this enabled me to form a personal connection by selling the candidates on us—our family, our children, our job, and our town—before I took the time to learn more about their qualifications and assess if *I* was interested in them. While the success of your efforts in selling the job to a strong candidate may not be immediately evident, your failure in this regard can readily be so.

Please note that I *never* misrepresented or candy-coated our position requirements in any phase of the interview, nor do I advocate that you do so. If there is something about your position or family that may be somewhat unconventional or complicated (a handicapped child, frequent overnight travel by parents, a divorce in process, etc.), you should be very direct about it in the early part of your conversation. For example, our family is Jewish. During our search, we spoke with several candidates from the rural Midwest and South where Jews are more of a rarity and may be subject to some preconceived notions. We mentioned our religion early in our conversations and expressly but delicately asked if it might make the candidate feel uncomfortable in our home. (We usually asked, "How would you feel about living in a house that was not decorated for Christmas—even if you could decorate your bedroom?") The answer was usually "no" (sometimes hesitantly and sometimes emphatically) but, one woman from Wyoming told me that she would be uncomfortable working for Jews and wanted to work for a Christian family. While it was somewhat surprising and painful to hear that sentiment, it was better that we found out before we spoke to her further and perhaps hired her, learning too late of her "preference."

Screening Family Day Care and Day-Care Centers

If you are considering an out-of-home childcare option, you will evaluate both the institution and the people who work there. In the case of a day-care center, you will screen with the director but also will interview the childcare providers. In the case of family day care, you will screen and interview the childcare provider (effectively the "director").

When you first identify a center about which you want to learn more, call and ask to speak with the director to do your screening. The director sets the tone for the center (much as a principal of a school or the proprietor of a store would) and ought to leave you with the impression that the center is professionally run as well as a loving and caring place for children to be. A well-run center ought to have a director who volunteers to answer questions over the telephone as well as send you printed materials (which you should of course accept willingly). Make sure that you take notes during your screening calls.

There are some key points that you will want to ascertain when screening a center. Look at your Candidate Qualifications and Job Description and determine which factors are most important to your selection. Among the points you should certainly cover are:

- What licenses and certifications does the center have? Ask to see the certificate or call the certifying agency to confirm the facts.

- What qualifications do your employees have?
- Are you affiliated with any religion, educational method, childcare philosophy?
- What age groups do you care for? What is the caregiver/child ratio?
- What are your hours and days of operation? Do you have extended care (early drop-off or late pickups)?
- What are your fees and what do they include?
- How long have you been in operation?
- Do you have a waiting list? How long is it?
- What is your policy on drop-in visits for prospective enrollees? Parents of enrolled children? **You should be permitted to drop in unannounced if your child is enrolled—this is a fundamental requirement to ensure the safety of your child.** Parents of enrolled children should *always* be able to drop in at *any* time (an open-door policy). For prospective enrollees, drop-ins for interviews may be restricted since it can be disruptive and take attention away from the children. On the other hand, you should be able to drop in to *observe* the center in action before you make an enrollment decision, although you will probably have to register at the office for security reasons when you arrive. **If a center does not maintain an open-door policy for parents of enrolled children, do not consider using that center—do not waste your time getting more information.**

If you have a positive first impression after this screening, find out when you can come in to meet the director and childcare providers to learn more. Plan on interviewing the caregiver who would be working *directly* with your child *and* observing them while working with the children. The interview conversations may be during your on-site visits or by telephone depending upon scheduling constraints.

At the same time that you contemplate scheduling your

on-site visits and interviews, ask for the names and telephone numbers of references for you to contact (see page 101, the chapter on checking references). Ideally, you should start checking these references *before* you make the on-site visit.

AFTER SCREENING

The Initial Interview

If you decide to interview a candidate, you may find that it is most efficient and productive to commence this by the telephone. The *initial interview* is intended to give you the opportunity to get to know the person or center better before deciding if you are interested enough to arrange for an on-site visit of a center or to invite an in-home caregiver to your home for an opportunity to meet you and your children.

The key to productive interviewing is a combination of a comfortable technique and well-drafted questions. By nature, interviewing is awkward—essentially you are asking prying questions of a virtual stranger while hoping that you are not being offensive. This is not easy for either party. During the interview process, you should try to maintain a friendly tone while being attuned to both the spoken and unspoken answers. We always kept our list of written questions (see page 87) on hand when we interviewed to ensure that we covered the major issues during the conversation. The questions would sound somewhat odd if posed outright ("Tell me about your relationship with your parents when you were growing up. What is your happiest memory? Describe your sense of humor."). Instead, they served as conversational guidelines (we also highlighted key points and ideas on the pages).

If possible, involve both parents in the interviewing process. You can interview jointly (if on the phone, use two extensions) or separately, depending on your style and preference. The point is that it is important that both parents are involved in the process of choosing the right childcare provider for their children.

The length and number of interviews with a candidate or center can vary depending on how well it is going and how quickly you are able to form your impressions of the person. My husband and I spent roughly an hour (after completing a screening) on a first interview for in-home caregivers. For those candidates that we liked and felt we needed to learn more about, we had a follow-up phone interview of another hour or so, then a face-to-face interview. For center-based caregivers, you may find that the interview will be less lengthy because the person has already passed an employment screening at the center and is not being considered to live or work in your home so certain issues need not be addressed (e.g., compatibility with your sleep schedule, etc.).

While much interviewing can be done by telephone, there are no substitutes for meeting the caregiver in person. I strongly endorse face-to-face interviewing before making a final decision to hire someone (or to place your child in a specific day-care program). This may be difficult if you are interviewing candidates who are not in your area (such as foreign au pairs). Unless you are willing to pay for round-trip transportation to your home for a face-to-face interview (in the case of foreign au pairs this may be particularly impractical), you will be interviewing only by telephone. Personally, especially while my children are young, I am firmly convinced that you cannot hire someone to care for your children unless you first "see the whites of their eyes." (I also would never buy a car until after a test drive, hire a contractor until I interviewed him in person, or marry someone until after we had dated.) Clearly, many families hire au pairs based solely on phone interviews and thus do not agree with this view, but this is the way I see it.

For center-based caregivers, you must be flexible about interviewing either during your on-site visit or over the telephone (although you should always observe the caregiver at work before you make a decision). During the interviews and in your on-site observations, assess whether each of the fundamental factors (the center, the director, and the caregivers) exhibit your essential Candidate Qualifications and can fulfill the Job Requirements that you have identified. Remember that center-based care is a package deal, so you should be favorably impressed with each of these factors (allowing, of course, some room for you to make those compromises we discussed earlier).

While I strongly advocate drop-in, or surprise, visits for center-based childcare, an *interview* requires that the individuals involved step away from their childcare responsibilities. That can be unfair to the children at the center so you need to be respectful of this and set up an appointment for a mutually convenient time.

Interview Questions

Our interview questions were divided into two basic categories—personal and job related—and focused on: (1) determining if the candidate met our qualifications, and (2) if they could fulfill the Job Requirements. Please note that many of the more personal questions are not be appropriate when you are speaking with a center-based caregiver because they do not work in your home. We also included a set of questions that involved hypothetical childcare situations to determine how the caregiver would respond. Because many of our Candidate Qualifications were subjective ("energetic," "creative," "common sense"), we had to think of questions that would elicit answers illustrating these qualities.

Our interview questions are listed below. *Keep in mind that these are intended to serve as ideas and outlines to guide your conversation during the screening and interview process rather than to serve as outright lines of inquiry.* The personal questions are best suited for in-home care while most of the job-related questions are applicable to all types of childcare arrangements.

EHRICH-ROSS INTERVIEW QUESTIONS

Job Related:
- What are your feelings about children?
- Why do/did you choose to be a caregiver?
- How did you find the job at this center?
- How long have you worked here? In this profession?
- How does this center compare to others in the area?
- How and when did your interest in this profession develop?
- Describe how you would spend a typical day with our children.
  ➤ Good weather/bad weather?
  ➤ Activities?
- What do you think are the three most important things for a child?
- How do you promote certain types of behavior?
- How do you believe that young children should be disciplined? Older children?
  ➤ Minor versus major infraction?
  ➤ Define "well behaved."
(Note: The following questions are oriented for the in-home caregiver.)
- Tell us about your previous childcare experiences.
  ➤ Ages/genders of children.

➤ What were your responsibilities?

➤ What activities did you do while watching the children?

➤ Have you ever spent a full day alone watching children?

➤ Have you ever baby-sat overnight?

➤ Have you ever driven the children somewhere as part of your job?

➤ Driving record and experience (city driving)?

➤ What were your favorite parts in those jobs?

➤ What were your least favorite parts?

• Why did you decide to attend nanny school (*or* get a childcare certificate, etc.)?

➤ What are your impressions of the school and the program?

➤ What is/was your living situation at school? How do you feel about it?

➤ What do/did you do with your free time at night? On weekends?

• What other types of jobs have you held (apart from childcare)?

➤ Responsibilities? Length of employment?

➤ What did you find most enjoyable? Dislike the most?

• Have you ever lived away from home before?

➤ Circumstances?

➤ How long?

➤ Have you ever been to our part of the country/ state? What are your impressions?

• Are you working now? Why are you thinking about leaving? May we talk with your current employer for a reference?

• How long would you like to stay in one childcare position?

• Why are you interested in the position we are offering?

- What are you looking for generally in a nanny position?
  - ➤ Children? Family? Work environment? Job content? Benefits?
- How do you feel about moving into a new home?
- Our job requires grocery shopping, starting dinner, and some errands. How do you feel about this?
- What questions do you have for us?
  - ➤ Children? Family? Town? State?

Personal: These are best suited for in-home caregivers.
- Tell us about yourself.
  - ➤ Personality: active/happy-sad/outgoing-quiet
  - ➤ Creativity
  - ➤ Flexibility
  - ➤ Neat-sloppy
  - ➤ How do you handle stress?
  - ➤ Best time of day?
- Describe your sense of humor . . . What do you think is funny?
- Do you have any hobbies or special interests that you presently pursue?
- What do you do for fun in your free time?
  - ➤ TV? Read? Phone? Exercise? Shopping? Church? Classes? Hobbies?
  - ➤ Do you have a boyfriend or any very close friends?
  - ➤ What are some of your favorite books/movies/TV shows?
- Describe yourself as a close friend would describe you.
- Describe yourself as someone who dislikes you might.
- How would your family (siblings/parents) describe you?
- Tell us about when you were a child.
  - ➤ Relationship with parents?
  - ➤ Relationship with sisters? Brothers? Other relatives?

➤ Happiest memory?

➤ Saddest memory?

➤ Favorite activities? Books? TV/movies? Music?

➤ Tell us about school. Grades? Activities? Awards?

- What was your hometown, your neighborhood, and your home like?
- When you misbehaved, how did your mother handle it? Father?

  ➤ How often were you physically disciplined?

  ➤ How do you feel about the way that you were disciplined?

  ➤ Is there anything that you would change?

- What is your own philosophy on discipline?
- Did you have a caregiver or go to day care when you were growing up? What did you think of the experience?
- What condition is your health?

  ➤ Allergies/asthma/cramps/migraines/other illness or conditions?

  ➤ Have you ever been hospitalized or treated for a major illness?

  ➤ Have you ever received counseling?

  ➤ What do you do to take care of yourself?

- How do you feel about moving to another part of the country? How does your family feel about it?
- How do you think you will spend your free time? Evenings? Weekends?
- What reservations do you have about our position?

How would you handle this childcare situation?
(These questions are suitable for all caregivers and arrangements.)

- Adam (the baby) wants to feed himself but he is very messy.
- Sam is playing outside and doesn't want to come in for the next activity.

- Adam wants to try to climb on the high bars of the jungle gym at the playground.
- Sam and Adam are fighting over a toy.
- You walk into the room and see that Sam is playing with an electrical outlet. He is upset that you caught him.
- Adam won't eat the snack or lunch you prepared for him; he wants a cookie/banana and yogurt/ice cream instead.
- Sam and Adam find a mud puddle in the yard and start to play together in it.
- Sam wants to go out to play and you tell him no because it is too cold. He has a tantrum.
- Sam and another child always seem to be getting into skirmishes.
- Adam refuses to go along with the planned activity on the schedule (e.g., nap time, outside play, etc.).

To compose your interview questions, start with a blank piece of paper and your Candidate Qualifications and Parenting Philosophy for guidance. How would you figure out what kind of person the candidate is? You could ask about her schooling, hobbies, life experiences, books read, movies seen, opinions on topical matters. Next, using your Job Requirements as a reference, write down questions that you would want to ask the person who cares for your child. You might ask about previous childcare experience, approach to children, discipline, her own childhood, etc. Whenever possible, use very open-ended questions (Why? How? What?) instead of those that require simple yes/no responses. At frequent intervals during the interview, pause and ask if the candidate has any questions for you.

After you have finished composing your questions, show them to some of your search resources (working-parent friends, agency contacts, etc.) for feedback. You want to be sure that you have covered all the important points, and feedback would be helpful on this point. Don't worry if someone tells you that you are asking "too much," you can and should selectively use these questions according to how the interview is going. Next, practice your interviewing technique on someone (your spouse, your contact at an agency, or an understanding friend—preferably a working mother). Solicit feedback on your technique; ask how you are coming across.

One last reminder (this is important), take notes as you interview a candidate and write down any final impressions or comments immediately after you finish. This will help you to remember what you did or did not like about that specific candidate and things that you learned about their skills and personal qualities.

Take comfort in knowing that everyone (except for personnel professionals) finds interviewing to be an intimidating process. Be prepared to stumble a bit in the beginning until experience polishes your technique, and remind yourself as often as needed: *I will look at many but I only need to find one.*

During the interview itself, be alert to how questions are answered as well as the answers themselves. You are looking for a demonstration that the candidate is truly interested in this position, such as an animated tone, making inquiries, etc. This is also an opportunity to assess some of the more amorphous qualifications such as creativity, common sense, and self-confidence. The content of the answers is also very important. You will be asking questions to see whether the candidate is in sync with your own parenting philosophy or specific skills requirements, and you know what responses you hope to hear. In the case of a center-based caregiver, you will have the opportunity to see her in action when you observe during the on-site visits. Compare what you see during your observation periods with the answers you are given during the interview.

Final Interview—Face-to-Face

Remember: Do not schedule a face-to-face interview until you have started to check all references and had positive feedback from them. (*Please* read chapter 7 on checking references, page 101, before you undertake this step—it is very important!) There is one exception to this process: centers that ask you to come in to meet the director, even in the early stages of your screening and initial interviewing process.

Face-to-face interviews are the best means of assessing a candidate's qualities as a childcare provider (short of hiring her). It is also the final step you take before choosing a center or making a job offer to a candidate. This personal meeting is not a fact-finding mission like the preceding interviews; it is more of a getting-to-know-you event. In this section, I will focus on suggestions for face-to-face interviewing of in-home caregivers. Chapter 8 (page 111) provides extensive guidance on face-to-face interviewing of center-based caregivers within the context of an on-site visit.

Telephone conversations and essays may reveal a great deal about a person—enough perhaps to eliminate someone from consideration—but you cannot truly assess the suitability and qualities of the individual until you see how they interact with your family, especially with your children. You cannot tell if someone truly enjoys playing with a child by having an adult conversation with them on the telephone, nor can you see if they have a patient disposition until they are seated for a meal with a toddler. In this life, you cannot choose your parents, but you can choose your spouse. The person you select to care for your children is the next most important choice you may make after that one.

The face-to-face interview permits you to see how reality compares to expectations: how everyone gets along, how your children react to the candidate and vice versa, and how the candidate reacts to you and your home/community. Even with all the preparation you have done up until this point and your positive impressions thus far, the candidate will not work out in the position if your family and she do not click. This is hard to determine fully over the telephone or on paper. After completing the initial round of interviewing a candidate for *at least* an hour *and* checking references, if you feel that this person is worth talking to further, invite the candidate for an interview in your home. My husband and I spoke to the live-in candidates for two to three hours by phone (often spread over three phone calls over a four- or five-day period during which time we also checked references) before we were able to determine if we wished to have a face-to-face interview. Since we were often interviewing long-distance candidates, the expense of transportation was high so we wanted to be judicious in extending invitations; for local candidates, this is not as much of a limitation.

The invitation to visit your home should be sincerely extended—you want to convey to the candidate that she is in serious contention for the position and that it is important that she likes you as much as you like her. (We usually said something like: "We have really enjoyed our conversations and hope you have too. We were hoping that you might want to visit us so that you could meet our children and get to know our home and community. . . .") With a local candidate, ask the person to join you for either a relaxed afternoon or lunch on the weekend and have her plan on spending three hours or more with your family. If possible, especially for a live-in position, ask if the candidate would like to arrive for lunch or dinner and "sleep over." For a long-distance candidate, plan on being host for at least one weekend night. (Clearly, with long-distance candidates, these interviews require more lead time since you have to arrange for transportation, etc.)

Upon her arrival in your home, keep in mind that the candidate will probably be somewhat nervous (because ideally, the person really wants the job and is anxious to please you). You might be nervous too (because you asked the candidate to visit with the hope that the person will like your situation enough to accept an offer should you make it). Your initial interviewing should have revealed a great deal about the candidate; now you are just trying to determine if there is a fundamental compatibility between your family and the individual.

Some key points to which you should be attuned during this visit are:

1. *Interaction with your child(ren)*: Provide ample opportunities for the candidate to interact with the children. Look for an excuse to leave the room while your children are still there. Wait and see if the candidate is truly interested in talking or playing with the children or if she acts only with your encouragement. Also, see how your children respond to the person. You know how your children normally behave around people with whom they are or are not comfortable. Children have a very good sixth sense about other people—observe their reactions and interactions, and take them seriously.

2. *Temperament and demeanor*: Does this person have the positive attributes that you would hope to see in someone who will be a big influence in the lives of your children? You should seek the qualities you want to find in a strong role model such as kindness, patience, sense

of humor, self-respect, etc. What weakness does the person seem to have? While the candidate is not applying to be your best friend, she should be someone with whom you can develop a mutual respect (and, if for a live-in job, can live with).

3. *Intelligence/common sense*: While it may be nice to find a childcare provider who can teach your child to speak in three foreign languages, you should focus more on whether you see any displays of good common sense and basic intelligence. Make sure that the candidate demonstrates that she has a good head on her shoulders.

4. *Work ethic/ability to take direction*: This is a bit hard to determine but it is important that the caregiver not only be smart enough to do what is requested but also that she is *willing* to do those things. In other words, you want to hire someone who will be a good employee. For example, I was always interested to see if the candidate offered to help set the table or started to help clear dishes after we ate or if instead she waited for me to be the busboy.

5. *Interest in position*: Does the candidate seem to be really interested in your childcare position? Be sensitive to the following signals: Even if she asked lots of questions in the initial interview, is she still making an effort to learn more about and become more comfortable with your family and community? Does she seem eager to make a positive impression on you? Is she enjoying her time with your children?

6. *Self-confidence, grooming, and overall presentation*: Does the candidate have enough self-respect to take care of herself? Don't dismiss a candidate who has a weight problem but is well groomed, polite, and pleasant (but do dismiss one who is unkempt, slovenly, or rude—especially knowing that this was an interview—or alternatively, very self-absorbed).

7. *Pet peeves*: Is there anything about this person that you find particularly upsetting? Is it something that you *really* cannot tolerate (such as coarse language or gluttony) or is it more of an annoying pet peeve that you can learn to live with (for example, using too much salt or collecting silly dolls)?

If the face-to-face interview is not going well due to shortcomings in any of the key points above or other issues, do not be shy about cutting it short. There is little point in wasting your time or the candidate's if the outcome is going to be negative anyway. Change the person's travel schedule for an earlier departure or, if that is not possible, let her watch TV and read in the guest room. Personal interviews are *supposed* to bring any problematic developments to the forefront before you make a hiring mistake.

My family's experiences are proof of the importance of the face-to-face interview. We put our money where our mouths were while conducting our search for a live-in nanny and, in the long run, it paid off. Firstly, we dismissed hiring an au pair from Europe solely because we could not interview the candidates in person before we hired. Then, following through on promising telephone interviews, we paid for several sets of train tickets and one set of plane tickets, so that we could have some of the candidates spend a weekend with our family. This step cost us money in the short run but saved us heartache in the long run. One candidate, for instance, talked incessantly about anything *but* our children or position, including her insomnia, her need to get a new place to live by the end of next week when her lease ended, and the midnight shift she worked at a convenience store. The following morning (Saturday), she slept until 10:00 A.M., when we finally woke her (a bad sign when interviewing for a job that has a 6:30 A.M. start time). By then, we had already checked the train schedules and found out that the next train to her hometown left in two hours. We told her that the chemistry was not right—no offense intended—packed her a box lunch and drove her to the station.

A second candidate displayed absolutely no interest in playing or talking with our children, had terrible eating habits, and asked us for a ride to a town forty minutes away so that she could pick up a used car that she was driving back home to a friend who was buying it from a cousin who happened to live in our area. Clearly, we were bamboozled (after we had bought her a costly round-trip train ticket).

A third candidate spent a very pleasant weekend with us, indicated that she would accept our job offer as she left, then called the next day to say that she decided she did not want to be a nanny anymore. (That one really set us back. . . .)

These were all people who had strong initial interviews and good (at least) to great references. In retrospect, there were probably signs during the telephone interviews. With more careful consideration and by not succumbing to a bit of desperation (yes, we had our moments of despair), we would not have scheduled these visits. But we did and fortunately they served their purpose by concretely demonstrating that these individuals were not the best candidates for our position.

Without face-to-face interviews, and given our state of mind at that point in our search, we might have extended a job offer to one of these candidates only to regret it after a few weeks or months. Moreover, these learning experiences focused us in the right direction so that we were able to recognize more quickly the best-quality candidate when she did come along. When our live-in nanny arrived in our home for her face-to-face interview, we could tell within the first two hours that she was perfect for our position. Our experiences in face-to-face interviewing convinced me of the importance of a seeing-the-whites-of-her-eyes meeting before hiring a caregiver for my children.

But This Just Isn't Working for Me. . . .

Please note that the purpose of the tasks outlined in this chapter and those that preceded it is to help you *find* childcare. Once you overcome any hesitation you may have in actually doing an interview, the process should become productive. If instead you are unable to find *anyone* who pleases you enough to be a *somewhat* viable candidate, then you need to step back and reexamine your preparation by considering the following questions:

1. Have I *really* accepted that I need to hire a caregiver for my child?
2. What was the problem with each of these people? Is there a common thread?
3. Am I looking for a quality or skill that I did not put on my list?
4. Am I being unreasonable in my unwillingness to compromise on Candidate Qualifications or Job Requirements?

If you cannot honestly answer yes to the first question, return to the discussion at the beginning of this book: until you accept that you need to find childcare, you will be setting yourself up for failure. However, if you have overcome this possible obstacle and are still not seeing the type of childcare providers that you want, think carefully about the other questions. You may need either to refine your Candidate Qualifications and/or Job Requirements or decide on additional areas of compromise. If the truthful answers to these questions is that you do not need to revise your qualifications/requirements or cannot compromise further, then you need to think about these questions:

- Am I conducting my search in the most productive way to find my "right" candidates? Am I looking in the right places with the most productive search resources?
- Am I targeting the type of childcare arrangement that matches my Candidate Qualifications? Are the Candidate Qualifications and Job Requirements compatible? Is my budget realistic?

You may need to go back to some of the preparatory stages before you can have a successful search.

CHAPTER 7

How to REALLY Check
References

IF YOU HAVE gotten to the point where you like a candidate or center enough to arrange for a personal face-to-face interview, take the time to check references first. Do so for *any* childcare arrangement that you might be considering (in or out of home), even if the candidate came very highly recommended from a close friend or relative and even if you are 100 percent certain that this is the right candidate for your position. Think of the rush you feel when experiencing love at first sight and the letdown that occurs once you see your beloved in the light of day. References complement the interview process by serving as a vital reality check. Keep in mind that checking references is about as much fun as interviewing, so you may find it necessary to remind yourself that you have a very important and worthy goal: finding the very best caregiver and arrangement for your child.

For a well-qualified candidate, the reference checks may serve to reinforce your impressions that this is a person worth considering further. However, you might learn of issues that did not come up in interviewing and which influence your impressions of the person. For a candidate who seems pretty good but not great, you may find that the reference check offers better insight into her personal qualities as a superb childcare provider (despite being a weak interviewee). At a minimum, references will provide you with more information to make an educated choice of childcare providers. As with interviewing, you should take notes so that you can recall the information you obtained when trying to make your final selection.

Human nature is such that people shy away from saying bad things about others, especially to strangers who call from out of the blue. When calling on a reference, keep this in mind and be gracious as you introduce yourself and explain the purpose of your call. ("My name is Michelle. I am considering enrolling my son in the Happy Days Center and Mrs. Director gave me your name as a reference." Or "I was given your name by Mary Smith as a childcare reference. Can you speak with me now or would you like to set up a more convenient time to talk?") Keep in mind that the reference person is doing you a favor by taking the time to speak with you. Nevertheless, don't be surprised if you sense some hesitance on the part of the reference to schedule a time to talk to you or say "unkind" things when you finally do speak. By asking open-ended questions and reading between the lines, you can assess this underlying sentiment as well as gain interesting feedback. Also, be sensitive to the fact that the reference may be trying to avoid speaking with you by not returning your calls or cutting the conversation short after you pose a sensitive question. A friend and former co-worker told me of her reluctance to call back a parent who wanted to check the reference of her children's former nanny ("Claire"). Several months earlier, Claire had moved out and disappeared while my friend's family was away for the weekend without having given any notice or mentioning her intentions to leave. After ascertaining that Claire had moved back in with her own family in a different state, my friend changed the locks on her doors and reported the incident to the police as a precaution. My friend had never been contacted by the agency now trying to place Claire (although evidently she had been noted as a former employer on the application) and she did not know how to break the news of Claire's flight to the parent who was now calling her. She chose not to return the call.

The manner in which you pose your reference questions should be informal and friendly rather than adversarial. Be well prepared so that the conversation is productive and you don't waste anyone's time.

CHECKING REFERENCES FOR IN-HOME CHILDCARE

When hiring an in-home childcare provider, you should check several *types* of references: two *work* related (including at least one childcare); two *personal* nonfamily; one *family* (usually parents but sometimes grown children if the candidate is older). In each case, you gain a different perspective on what the candidate is like as a person and her strengths and weaknesses.

- *Work:* General attitude and work ethic; ability to take direction and perform; personality; maturity; childcare abilities including interaction with children, responsibility, energy level, etc.
- *Personal (nonfamily):* Personality; hobbies; background; type of friend the candidate is.
- *Family:* Background; influences on personality; values; nature of relationship with parents and siblings; supportiveness of parent(s); type of child (or parent).

If you are working with a quality agency, it should have already checked all of the references and provided them to you in writing. (Reminder: Do not use an agency that does not do this minimum level of screening.) This is helpful but it is not a substitute for doing it yourself. Previous employers are sometimes especially reluctant to say unfavorable things about a caregiver to an agency, while they might be somewhat more open with you as a fellow parent. I confirmed this quirk of human nature when checking the reference of a prospective nanny who was very highly regarded by an agency. All the references checked by the agency were positive and the nanny's first manager also gave me a glowing reference. I was surprised when the most recent employer reluctantly confided in me that she felt the candidate was lazy because the nanny had made her five-year-old take daily naps so that she too could nap and the house was often left a mess (*really* a mess—she gave me the details!), which the mother had to clean when she returned from work.

Our reference questions were somewhat tailored to reflect the different perspectives of the references (work, personal, family). Use our questions as a guideline to formulate your own and remember to incorporate the following points:

1. Verify the facts to ensure that it is a legitimate reference. Unfortunately, false references are more common for in-home childcare providers than for family day care or day-care centers. There are instances of relatives or friends posing as former employers, etc. By obtaining several work references and being sensitive to this issue as you ask questions, you should be able to detect any problems of this nature. Clearly, if there is a false reference given, you should cease to consider the candidate as a viable prospect.

2. Description of strengths and weaknesses, personality and interests.
3. Quality of work performed.
4. "Would you hire her again?" "Would you have any reservations about rehiring her or providing a recommendation for *our* childcare position?" These few questions are the most revealing and useful of any you can ask. Always include them in your reference checking.

Below are the questions that we kept on hand as we checked references. We did not ask each reference to answer all of them but found them very helpful guidelines in keeping the conversation on track when we spoke. These questions are most helpful when hiring in-home caregivers. You can also use some of these for family day care.

REFERENCE QUESTIONS
Note: It is uncommon, but a candidate may provide false references. It is important first to verify that it is a legitimate reference by confirming some of the background facts you may have. One way to verify is to make deliberate misstatements and wait to be corrected. You can also do this by asking open-ended questions to which you already know the answers.

General Reference
(For all types of references)

How do you know the candidate?
Describe her to me.
What are her best qualities?
What areas do you feel need improvement?
Rate on a scale of 1–10 (10 is highest):
➤ Work ethic?
➤ Flexibility?

➤ Maturity?
➤ Common sense?
➤ Sense of humor?
➤ Disposition?
➤ Self-confidence?

Childcare Reference

What sorts of activities did she do with your children?
What do your children think of her?
Did she ever have to:
➤ drive your children anywhere?
➤ watch them overnight?
➤ prepare meals?
➤ handle a disruption of plans (e.g., expected to do something but the weather was bad)?
➤ handle an emergency?
How much supervision did you have to provide?
Would you hire her again for your job? (This is the *best* question.)
Would you recommend her for a nanny position? Do you have any reservations?

Other Work Reference

Length of employment?
Job requirements?
What kind of worker was she? (Prompt? Well groomed? Healthy? Friendly? Professional? etc.)
Level of responsibility given?
Willingness to accept responsibility? (Did just what was required? More? Less?)
Would you hire her again? Why?
How would you rate her qualifications for our position?

Family and Personal References

How long have you known her?

Describe her as a child to me.

Did she become the sort of adult you envisioned she would be?

If she were not related to you, would you choose to be her friend? Why?

How do you feel about her choice of profession?

How do you feel about the prospect of her moving far from home and family for a position?

➤ How do you think she will do being far from home?

➤ Are you generally comfortable or uncomfortable with this situation?

➤ Do you have any questions or concerns for us to respond to?

Would you hire her for this position in your home?

Would you recommend her for this position in our home?

Do you have any reservations?

Your own references questions should be open-ended in nature, much like those in a candidate interview. It sounds simplistic but try to use the words "why," "how," and "what" and to avoid yes/no questions—it really works! The questions should be oriented toward how the reference person reacted to the candidate rather than asking the person to project him- or herself into your own situation. These two factors will result in questions that yield more productive responses as well as circumvent some of the reference's reluctance to say explicitly bad things about another person. For example, rather than asking "Would you recommend Beth as a nanny?" or "Do you think Mary has the qualifications to be a good caregiver?" instead ask "If you had the opportunity to hire Beth again as your child's nanny, would you, and why?" and "What qualifications induced you to choose Mary as your child's caregiver? What reservations did you have?'' Lastly, be sensitive to *how* things are said (or not said)—it can be as meaningful as what you are being told. *Don't forget to take notes!*

Once you finish *personally* checking all the references of a prospective candidate (or center), you should have a very good idea of whether your own impressions of the person are accurate and if this individual is truly a viable candidate. Only *after* doing this should you arrange for a face-to-face interview (if at all possible) or the on-site visit.

CHECKING REFERENCES FOR FAMILY DAY CARE OR DAY-CARE CENTERS AND THE QUESTIONS YOU SHOULD ASK

Ask the director for the names of at least two current and two former clients to check as references. Try to obtain at least one reference who has or had an enrolled child the *same* age as your own who was with the *same* caregiver you are considering. When you get their names and phone numbers/addresses, also ask for some general background of the references such as number of children in family, names, length of enrollment, reason for leaving, etc.

Inquire also about contact names and phone numbers at professional organizations, accreditation agencies, and governmental licensing agencies. These are more business-like references, comparable to those you might check if you were hiring a construction contractor or a moving company. Your reference questions in these instances should focus upon whether the center is in good standing, its rating (if any), its record regarding complaints received at the agency and their resolution.

Following are some suggested points that you should cover once you schedule the time to speak with an individual reference (these questions can be easily adapted for both current or former enrollees).

1. Verify that this is a legitimate reference by confirming some of the background facts you were given by the center. It is uncommon, but a center may provide false references. You can do this by asking open-ended questions to which you have already been given answers. ("How old was your son when he began to attend Happy Days? How long was he enrolled?")
2. How did you first learn of Happy Days? What attracted you to the center initially? What other centers did you consider? Why did you end up choosing Happy Days?
3. How did you feel about the quality of the care your child received? The quality of the facilities? How did you feel about the childcare providers?
4. What are the strengths of Happy Days' program? What do you think are the three biggest weaknesses of the program?
5. What aspect of the center or its staff would you have changed? What suggestions can you offer for improvements at Happy Days?
6. Why did your child stop attending Happy Days? (Check the facts.) Were there any factors that, if different, would have led you to reconsider your decision? What were they?
7. Would you enroll your child at Happy Days again? Why?
8. Would you recommend Happy Days to your best friend or a close relative?
9. Do you have anything else to add or bits of advice?

If during your preparation phase you have identified specific or unique requirements or qualifications that are of particular importance to you, be sure that you ask about these when you check the references. For example, if low employee turnover is a key requirement of yours, ask "How many different childcare providers did your child have while enrolled at Happy Days?"

CHECKING DRIVING RECORDS, POLICE RECORDS, AND CREDIT AGENCIES

In addition to checking references, you need to make sure that the prospective caregiver does not have any undisclosed black marks in her past such as a shoplifting arrest or suspended license. This can be difficult to do on your own since you need to have access to the data sources in addition to signed consent from the candidate. A licensed day-care center should do this before hiring any personnel (caregivers or administrative); confirm this point when you speak to the director. If you are using a quality employment agency, it should do this for you and provide you with the written results. (If not, you should not use the agency.)

If you have found a candidate or unlicensed center by word of mouth or through the classified ads, it is more difficult, although not impossible, to check these points on your own by hiring an agency that specializes in these types of investigations. You can find these services by asking a good employment agency to refer one to you or by checking in the Yellow Pages under Investigators. The only instance when I would *maybe* forgo having this type of checking done is if I am hiring someone who I either already know well or whose references I already know very well.

In sum, checking references is a valuable and essential tool in the search for quality childcare. No search is complete without this vital component.

CHAPTER 8

On-Site Visit of Out-of-Home Childcare Locations

THE ON-SITE VISITS to an out-of-home childcare facility is essential before you can make your final selection. During your visits, you will be conducting the face-to-face interviews with the caregivers (see chapter 6) in addition to assessing the environment and overall facilities. Keep in mind that centers are a package deal and *each* component of the package (the caregivers, the facility, the environment) must meet your standards. Regardless of how attractive or appealing the center may seem, if the caregivers who will be with your children do not meet your standards (or vice versa), then this is not the right choice for you.

Please note that I intentionally use the plural *visits*. If you are seriously considering a particular center, you should visit it on different occasions and at different times of day, both with and without an appointment, to get a feel for what the environment is truly like.

Your reference checks will make your on-site visits more productive by sensitizing you to matters that were of concern (or appreciated) by other parents. Remember that you can take the liberty of calling a reference again if the on-site visit raised new questions in your mind. (Please note that if you are unable to complete your initial interview by phone with the director, it may warrant waiting until after your first on-site visit/interview before you begin to call on references.)

THE ON-SITE VISIT: WHAT IS THE ENVIRONMENT LIKE?

The objective of the on-site visit for both family day care and day-care centers is to assess critically the environment and the quality of the childcare offered through observation (much like in the face-to-face interview of an in-home caregiver). This may seem a daunting task but it comes down to answering this simple question as you tour the center and speak to the caregiver: "If I were my child, would I want to spend my day here?"

Keep in mind that the center environment is not a home and may often be institutional in appearance. That does not mean the center-based care is bad, only that expectations and reality sometimes diverge. "Institutionality" is a frequent fact of center-based childcare and it is worthwhile to note what efforts that center has made to make the physical plant more homey or warm. Also, just because it is not a homelike setting, it does not mean that your child must forgo comfort, safety, cleanliness, or "wholesomeness" in a day-care center.

During your first on-site interviews (i.e., with the director, etc.) as you tour the facility, stop by the group/room where your child would be placed. Ask if you can observe some of the childcare providers at work (especially the ones who would be caring for your child) and plan on spending at least a half hour doing so. Make a special effort to observe the caregivers in action during each of your visits (announced and unannounced), although the half-hour commitment is not always needed. If at any time you are not permitted to observe, find out why; this is highly unusual and should be a cause of concern. (Recognize of course that if it is naptime, a peek into the room may suffice. Plan on observing during subsequent visits.)

Don't be shy about taking notes as you interview people, observe caregivers in action, and tour the facility (also write down your general impressions when you leave); this will help you when you make your final choice. Some of the issues that should be covered during your visits include the following.

Structure of Day/Activities

Ask how your child will be spending the day. Quality daycare centers have programs that set aside time for a variety of activities. For toddlers (up to twenty-four months), an appropriately structured day might consist of the following (with the understanding that young children often move at their own pace):

- 7:15–8:15   drop-off and quiet play/story time
- 8:15–9:00   breakfast and circle time
- 9:00–10:15   in- or outdoor free play, outings, or special programs
- 10:15–10:45   light snack and story/quiet time
- 10:45–11:45   nap or rest time
- 11:45–12:15   lunch
- 12:15–2:00   indoor programs (crafts/singing/etc.)
- 2:00–3:00   in- or outdoor free play, stroller ride, or special programs
- 3:00–4:00   nap/rest time
- 4:00–4:30   light snack
- 4:30–6:00   story/quiet time until pickup

The general idea is that the environment ought to be stimulating, age appropriate, and fun for your child. For example, older preschoolers might have a schedule with less nap/rest time and more early learning opportunities, while infants may have more nap time scheduled. When you drop in, check to see what the children are doing and if it differs from the schedule, find out why.

Family day care (especially for small groups of three or fewer children) is often less structured in its day. Some parents may find this more casual approach to be appealing (I did since I felt that babies should not live by the clock); others do not like this free-form nature. The trade-off of having less structure should be that the children get more individualized attention and schedules, in a more homelike setting, and more opportunities to get out into the world (trips to the supermarket, etc.).

Family day care should be nurturing and attentive to each child's unique needs. It is not "watching" children in the literal sense (i.e., the children sit around and the caregiver watches them sit around). Beware of a family day-care setting that always has a TV on, has very few toys available or in use, and in which the children seem to be unattended or wandering aimlessly around the house. When my children were in family day care, their primary activities (aside from meals and naps on their own schedules) consisted of playing (inside and out) and taking "excursions" (the drugstore, the school playground, the supermarket, etc.) that were exciting for them. It was a very relaxed, child-oriented environment and they enjoyed themselves.

Philosophical, Educational, or Religious Affiliation

Many centers are affiliated with religious or educational organizations. Even an informal family day-care setting reflects at least the child-rearing outlook of the caregiver. While you may not have to be a member of the same religion to send your child to an affiliated center, you should be comfortable with the nature of the content of the programs offered. For example, because we are Jewish, I was not comfortable with day-care programs that were aggressively Christian in nature (e.g., with daily religion programs or crosses on the walls). On the other hand, I had no problem considering centers housed in churches as tenants but with which their programs were not affiliated.

Some centers are affiliated with or subscribe to specific educational philosophies (e.g., Montessori). Make sure that you understand how that affiliation affects their outlook and program and that you are comfortable with the general approach. For example, there is a well-regarded quality day-care center in my area that is a "developmental center." Part of the philosophy is that children can learn from each other as well as from adults. The program places children of various ages within a range in small groups to promote learning and socialization. There is an infant/toddler room, for example, where children are placed in small groups of four each with a range of ages (six weeks to twenty-four months) and one caregiver for each mixed group.

Parenting Philosophy

It is vital that you are in sync with the center's parenting philosophy and practices. Find out where the center stands on issues that are of major importance to you, and how the childcare providers convey these beliefs, both in theory and in practice. Among the points to consider are discipline, values, role of children, etc. For example:

- If your child is crying, do you believe that she should be comforted immediately, allowed to explore her own solutions for a bit and then comforted, or encouraged to solve her own problems without adult intervention?

- At what age do you feel it is important for your child to learn "manners," and how would you teach these things (such as taking turns, eating with utensils, not interrupting, etc.)?
- When do you think a child should be toilet trained and how?
- What values do you want to teach to a child at this age?
- What do you feel are the most effective means of discipline for children?
- What is the desired level of parental involvement? Some centers ask parents to participate by spending time each month to read a story or to do weekend maintenance work or by participating in fund-raising activities. Can you and would you do this?
- How much tolerance is there for expressions of individuality? Some children thrive in a structured environment with lots of direction and others prefer to live in their own world. How does the center handle a child who is a loner or does not like to participate in group activities?

Chances are that you will not agree with everything that the center practices or believes but you ought to agree on the major issues and not find any to be fundamentally offensive or unacceptable. One unique advantage in assessing the parenting philosophy of family day care is that you may have the opportunity to witness the outcome in practice by observing the caregiver's own children, their attitudes, and their behavior.

Communication

How will you as the parent be kept abreast of what your child is doing during each day? Is there a notice board that gives the highlights of each day every day or a weekly newsletter? Does the caregiver send home individual notes or progress reports on a regular basis? Are there parent-caregiver conferences, and how frequent are they? Is there time at the start or end of each day for a few words to be exchanged with the caregiver? Especially with younger children, you need to have access to the caregiver and director to find out what is going on. A quality day-care center has all of the items noted above. For family day care, communication is more informal but still important. Determine that the caregiver is willing and able to spend a few moments or so every day when you pick up your child to discuss what went on and how things are going.

Child Orientation

This ought to be an obvious point: Of course, the center should be child oriented! But to really know if this is the case, you should try to look at the facilities and programs from the point of view of your child—even if that means getting on the floor and crawling around (really). How does the world look from down there? Is it stimulating, safe, fun, and comfortable, or is it frustrating, uninteresting, uncomfortable, and dangerous? For example, some day-care centers are physically located in multipurpose facilities (such as a church gym or basement) that may not be accommodating to the needs of children of a certain age (hard floors, high windows, etc.) unless adaptations are made to make it more appealing.

Some family day-care homes are also not child friendly—comparable to when your child is a tolerated guest in the home of a childless family. I visited one family day care that had a huge deck and a lovely backyard, and was situated across the street from a town park. The deck had safety gates (which was good) but I noticed no children's toys or equipment in the yard. When I inquired, the childcare provider told me that the children were not allowed to leave the deck and that they never went across the street for outings in the park. Although all the elements were there to enrich a child-oriented environment, they were consciously not being used, as if it were inconvenient, and I found that to be a telling indication. On the other hand, when I visited the family day care that we used after Sam was born, the living room was a delightful jumble of laundry baskets and stuffed animals. The caregiver's children had set up a "zoo" that morning and clearly had a controlled run of the house in doing so. Finally, I recall one visit to an infant and baby day-care center where the sound level was unbearable. Children were wailing in their cribs and there simply were not enough hands or laps to comfort them. The director kept speaking to me as she shuffled papers on her desk in the front of the infant room (I guess she had learned to tune out the noise). I was surprised that she did not take a moment to put one of the babies on her knee for a jiggle as we spoke. After all, if she did not stop to attend to the children while I was there watching, what happened when I was not there? I left the center knowing that I could never put my infant there. Every time you visit a center, make the effort to be especially attuned to these signs.

Rules and Requirements

Family day care and day-care centers all have rules and requirements in order to prevent any misunderstandings and to ensure that the facility continues to run smoothly. Day-care centers tend to have formal written rules that cover many points such as hours of operation and penalties for late pickups, child sickness policy, fees, disciplinary methods, food and diaper requirements. Most rules will also contain explanations of the philosophy of the program, the procedures for handling complaints regarding staff or programs, and penalties for noncompliance with the rules. Make sure you read, understand, and can live with these rules since they are often nonnegotiable.

Family day care often does not have written rules. In such cases, ask the caregiver to clarify the ground rules in order to prevent any misunderstandings. One of the advantages of family day care is that it does tend to offer more flexibility, so don't be surprised if there are very few restrictions or details. Still, it is important that both you and the caregiver are on the same wavelength when it comes to the basic parameters in caring for your child and the basic operation of the center.

Staffing—Ratio, Turnover, Training, Qualifications

The ratio of caregivers to children is an important factor that directly influences the quality of care that you can expect your child to receive. Maximum ratios are usually specified in licensing requirements, however you may decide that such a number is too high to allow individualized attention and nurturing. Call the licensing agency to find out what these mandated ratios are. You can then determine if the center meets or exceeds them, regardless of whether they are licensed.

Clearly, the older the children, the higher the caregiver:child ratio can be. For infants, I believe that the ratio ought to be in the 1:3 or 1:4 (maximum) range or lower, regardless of the licensing standards. For toddlers (eighteen to thirty-six months), I believe that 1:4 to 1:7 could be acceptable (depending upon the actual ages of the children).

Aside from asking about the ratio, observe it in action. If the center tells you that the ratio in the infant room is 1:3, check during your unannounced visits to see if that is the fact. If the ratio is higher (either more children or fewer staffers than you had been told), ask what happened. If there is a staff illness, are there substitutes available? Does the center permit parents to drop off children without "reservations" so that it cannot plan for appropriate coverage? This concern holds true for family day care as well. The provider in one family day care I had visited (and which was fully licensed by the state) told me that her mother assisted her during the day (they advertised themselves as a "mother-daughter team"). Although she complied with all the state licensing ratios even without having her mother there, I was attracted to the fact that there was an extra pair of hands to help out and play with the children. Unfortunately, during *both* of my unannounced drop-in visits, the mother was *not* there. I made my decision to dismiss this home as a viable prospect because of that lack of reliability.

Staff turnover can be unfortunately high at some day-care centers. (This is often correlated to the level of compensation paid to the staff and can serve as a warning sign regarding the quality of the care.) High turnover can be problematic because you want both your child and yourself to know and have a good relationship with the caregiver, and frequent changes in caregivers can be traumatic and disruptive for young children. Ask the director about this topic in a very direct fashion. Find out if there are any programs to retain good employees (raises, incentives, and so on). If a center has high turnover, it should be a cause for concern.

Quality day-care centers should be proud to answer your questions about their employee qualifications and their hiring process. (Note: make sure that someone on staff is trained in basic first aid for children). Additionally, ask if the center offers any ongoing training to its caregivers so that they can maintain their standards of performance and enthusiasm for their work. This is a nice perk but not many centers do it. You want to make sure that the objective of the center is to hire caregivers who are qualified and want to work with children, not just adults who want to work, period (meaning at any job they can get). Ask directly if the center checks all prospective employee references in addition to any police or driving records. These checkings should apply to everyone who works at the center, such as custodial staff, not just those who have direct contact with the children.

Licensing, Certification, Insurance, and Professional Memberships

Quality day-care centers should have the applicable state and local licenses/certifications and insurance required in your area. See the paperwork, confirm that it is current, and ask what standards and requirements must be met and maintained in order to obtain them. This may include everything from physical facility and safety standards to staff qualifications/training and ratios. Also, find out if the center is a member of any professional organizations, such as the National Association for the Education of Young Children (NAEYC); if so, it may have to uphold additional quality standards and offer a certain caliber of programs. Please note that having licenses, etc., does not mean that the day-care center is good, although not having them may be a warning sign that something is amiss.

Family day care may or may not be specially licensed or insured. Again, having licenses or special insurance, etc., is a good sign, but in these types of arrangements, lack of it is less telling. In many states, the requirements for family day-care licensing/certification can very difficult for a home-based business to meet (and perhaps unnecessarily high) such as fire extinguishers and exit plans posted in each room. If you perform a thorough examination of a family day-care home for safety, cleanliness, and overall environment, you could become comfortable that it meets your own standards (likely to be comparable to those in your own home) and find that it is acceptable even without a license. It is up to you to decide if you are comfortable with an unlicensed family day-care facility.

In a perfect world, all childcare providers would be fully licensed to do their jobs. However, in the real world where we all reside, the facts can be different. You will find that most day-care centers have whatever minimum level of licensing is needed to conduct business. However, there are professional certifications, for example from NAEYC, that can be difficult or time consuming to obtain and thus are not sought by many day-care centers. (Of course, extra credit should go to those that do make the effort.) Moreover, while some family day-care providers have some type of licensing (usually from the health and fire departments), many more do not. This is generally a reflection of the convoluted regulations that can govern this type of home-based business or of the preference of the family day-care provider to be paid in cash.

Insurance

Anyone who provides center-based childcare should have insurance coverage, even if the center is not licensed. **It is strongly recommended that the reader review all these issues with her own insurance agent.** The following are some points to be considered: If your child is being transported by the caregiver, you must confirm that there is valid auto insurance, either commercial or personal as applicable. An unlicensed family caregiver should have at least homeowners insurance, and preferably with an umbrella liability policy as well. A licensed center must have whatever insurance is required by the licensing authority. At a minimum, this should include property insurance (e.g., for fire, damages, etc.), a general liability policy with a professional liability endorsement (this is comparable to medical malpractice insurance), workers' compensation insurance, and of course, auto insurance (regular and/or commercial if applicable).

Fees

You need a clear understanding of the fee structure at the center. This includes payment requirements such as amounts, deposits, due dates, policies on payments during vacation or illness, etc. Know what the fee includes *and* excludes—such as meals, enrichment classes, trips, and so on. (If snacks and/or meals are included, be sure to review recent menus to see if they are nutritious and appealing.) Lastly, some centers offer discounts to families if siblings are enrolled; be sure to inquire if this applies to your family situation.

Cleanliness

Does the facility look and smell clean? If it does not pass this preliminary test, leave immediately; if it does, check to see if the center is clean. Do caregivers and children wash hands after changing diapers or using the bathroom? Is the eating area cleaned up between meals? Is the crafts area cleaned up after activities? Are conditions in the bathrooms, kitchen, and changing area sanitary? Are the children "well-kept"? (This is a relative term, of course, within the realm of kids who should be having fun indoors and out.) Are the toys clean and functional? Keep these points in mind when you drop in as well.

Roominess

Quite simply, this is an assessment of whether the center has sufficient space to accommodate comfortably the number of children enrolled and their varied activities The *ideal* physical layout should offer several activity centers: one for eating/crafts (messy activities), one for resting, one for quiet play (stories, etc.), and active play areas indoors and outdoors. These need not be separate rooms but rather can be clearly defined parts of a single space. For example, a room for four-year-olds might have a large carpeted area that serves as the quiet play space; nap time could also take place here on folding mats. Eating and/or craft tables may be in the indoor play area provided it is not overly crowded. There can be other acceptable compromises. These spaces also should exist in a family day care (e.g., eating and crafts in kitchen; napping in bedroom; indoor playing in rec room or den; outdoor playing in fenced yard). The point is to ensure that there is enough space for the children to be able to enjoy their days comfortably.

Safety and Security

This is a self-explanatory and familiar topic to most parents, but here are some reminders:

- gate or door at entrances to kitchen and bathrooms
- electrical outlet covers
- age-appropriate toys and furniture in good condition (no small parts, rough edges, shaky construction)
- cleaning products and medical supplies out of reach of children
- security of the facility (for a day-care center, it would mean daily sign-in/sign-out sheets and a control point that sees everyone who comes in to the center)
- fenced-in, fully visible outdoor play area

Ask the director about safety and security measures in place and have her point out these items during your tour. The safety standards at most centers that I visited exceeded those in my home (!); while that made me feel somewhat insecure about my own house, it made me more comfortable with the facilities I saw.

Specific Considerations for Your Situation

There is a possibility that your child may have one or two specific issues that must be addressed in the day-care setting. Some examples include:

- If your daughter has a severe peanut allergy, will the snack or meal menu meet her needs? Some such allergies are so severe that even the smell of peanuts can cause a reaction. How will the center let other parents of children in the group know of this matter and monitor it?
- Does your child have to take medication every day? Is the center willing and able to administer it? How will this be handled?
- If your son is afraid of swimming and the center offers a weekly swim class, what will he do during that time? Will he be forced to try it, sit and watch his group, or go in another group during that hour?

Make the effort to identify and address these issues in advance. During your visit, talk through the potential solutions and then walk through them to see if you are comfortable with the process. Most centers will try hard to accommodate relatively minor concerns, however some are not equipped or able to do so without disruption or difficulty.

A few day-care centers are truly superlative and will be outstanding in each of the areas noted above. I sincerely hope that you are able to find them. However, it is more likely that you will see a few very bad day-care centers and family day-care homes and many others that are satisfactory and above average in the areas outline above, with some areas being really outstanding and none being unacceptable. The key is to ensure that the outstanding qualities are those that are of most importance to you as a parent. As you complete each visit, your instinct will tell you if the center or home has the right outstanding qualities to make it a standout choice for your child.

Making a Choice and an Offer

You ARE NOW in the position of finishing your search for quality childcare and making a decision as to who will be the childcare provider for your child. By narrowing down your choices through compromising, screening, interviewing, and reference checking, you probably know already which candidate/center is the right choice for your child. If not, sort and review the notes you have accumulated for each candidate/center during the interviewing and reference-checking process. This alone may help you to identify the front-runner. If instead you are still undecided, write down the strengths and weakness of each candidate and compare them to your Candidate Qualifications and Job Requirements (revised to reflect the compromises you have been making). The best-qualified candidates will emerge.

WHAT IF I HAVE HIT A DEAD END?

What if the best candidate is still not good enough for you to consider hiring? While the quality of the candidates really may be the problem, there are probably other reasons for having hit this dead end. Ask yourself the following questions.

- Why do I feel that I am ready to stop searching for quality childcare and need to make my choice now? Am I running out of time? Am I getting desperate?
- Have I *truly* accepted the reality that I work and thus need to find quality childcare?
- Is there a common thread that is causing me to reject all the candidates/centers that I have reviewed? What were the problems?
- Have I selected the appropriate arrangement to meet my Candidate Qualifications and Job Requirements?
- Do my Candidate Qualifications and Job Requirements match the reality of my budget? Did I make productive compromises?
- Have I conducted my search in the most productive way to locate the quality childcare arrangement I am seeking?
- Have I devoted enough time and energy to this search or am I expecting results too quickly?

Be truthful with yourself as you respond. Most likely you need to go back a few steps in this process and pick up the search again with a renewed and/or redirected focus.

WRITTEN AGREEMENTS WITH IN-HOME CHILDCARE PROVIDERS

If you have decided to use in-home childcare, I strongly recommend that you document the arrangement in an agreement that both the nanny and the employers (you and your spouse) sign. The agreement serves several purposes:

- it demonstrates that you take this job and its responsibilities seriously;
- it instills a sense of professionalism and mutual respect into an employment relationship that tends to be somewhat informal;
- it clearly establishes all the job duties and requirements as well as any standing house rules;
- it specifies the job compensation and benefits.

All of the points in the agreement should have been conveyed to the candidate during the interviewing process so that nothing should come as a surprise. Nevertheless, it is worthwhile to put these items in writing today so that in six months you are not bickering about whether Columbus Day is a paid holiday for the caregiver, or who is responsible for loading and emptying the dishwasher after lunch. These little conflicts can fester and cause hard feelings that sour a working relationship just as quickly as a major job performance issue. In sum, while not a legal document, the written agreement is a very simple way to make expectations and obligations known and understood before the caregiver starts her job; such clarity can only help to make your relationship a success.

We wrote our own agreement. If you have used an employment agency, it might provide one to use (it may even require that both you and the nanny sign it). Given my own penchant for detail, our agreement is quite specific, perhaps overly so. You can easily be far more general than we have been (a simplified contract is also in Appendix F). Nonetheless, at the minimum, your contract should contain an overview of the following points:

- employment term
- work schedule: days and hours (including weekly "scheduling" conferences, etc.)
- duties and responsibilities (general and some specific) including childcare

- living arrangements (as applicable): accommodations provided; meals; car; visitors; responsibilities
- salary and benefits: salary amount and when paid; performance reviews; holidays and vacation (paid or unpaid?); sick days, if any; other compensation or benefits (air fare, educational stipend, etc.)
- house rules (most should apply to everyone in the house) such as no smoking, etc.
- notice to terminate

The following is a very simple version of a nanny agreement. It is followed by the format of the very detailed one that we used in our own childcare arrangement.

SAMPLE
CONTRACT FOR NANNY SERVICES
(SIMPLIFIED VERSION)

Nanny:

Mary Poppins

Family:

The Smith Family

Employment Period:

July 1, xxxx to June 30, xxxx

Hours and Days of Service:

Monday through Friday from 7:00 A.M. until 6:00 P.M. with additional hours as arranged plus one Saturday evening per month.

Responsibilities:

1. All childcare responsibilities related to the needs of Sam and Adam during the hours and days of service including:
   - interactive play; help with homework
   - proactive arrangement and transportation to activities and appointments including but not limited to weekly library trips, sporting activities, enrichment programs, etc.
   - bathing; laundry; preparing and feeding meals and snacks during the day
   - keeping all household common areas, children's rooms, and play areas clean and tidy
2. The following guidelines shall apply at all times:
   - no physical discipline
   - one hour of educational TV or videos per day and only after chores, bathing, homework, and creative play time are completed
   - visual supervision of children
3. Other responsibilities include the following:
   - grocery shopping and putting away all groceries
   - family laundry and folding
   - commence preparation of evening meal for family
   - doing local errands (e.g., dry cleaners, etc.)

Compensation:

- Weekly salary of $XXX to be paid every Friday.
- Ten days' vacation must be coordinated with our family plans for vacation.
- Six legal paid holidays: New Year's Day, President's Day, Memorial Day, July 4th, Thanksgiving Day, and Christmas Day.
- Use of car for job-related and personal reasons. Note: From time to time, we will need the car; we will try to

give you as much notice as possible in these cases. If there is any damage to the car or excessive gas usage or maintenance requirements, you are required to reimburse us for such costs.

- Private bedroom and telephone line. Note: You are responsible for keeping your room clean, paying for any damage or excessive wear to the room or its contents, and for the costs of all toll calls made.

House Rules:

- No smoking in our home or cars, or in front of our children.
- Please let us know if you plan on having guests visit you in our home.
- No food or beverages to be consumed outside of the kitchen.
- No personal calls or visits while on duty.

Termination of Agreement:

This agreement may be terminated by either party by providing four weeks' notice to the other. Recession can take place in a lesser period by mutual consent or if the terms of this contract are violated. This agreement may be amended by mutual consent only.

The undersigned agree to the terms, duties, and schedule as described above.

Employee   Date

Employer   Date

Nanny:

Mary Poppins

Family:

The Smith Family

The following agreement describes the expected schedule, duties to be performed, living accommodations, house rules, salary, duration of employment, and other miscellaneous items associated with the employment of Mary Poppins as a nanny for the Smith family.

EMPLOYMENT TERM

Employee will begin work on July 1, xxxx, for a period of one year.

WORK SCHEDULE

The expected working hours are 7:00 A.M. to 6:00 P.M., Monday through Friday, plus one Saturday evening monthly (for four to five hours) with all other Saturdays, every Sunday, prearranged vacation days, and specified legal holidays off. In addition, we require that you spend approximately thirty minutes with us on the weekend at a mutually agreeable time (usually Sunday evening) so that we can go over the schedule for the upcoming week. We expect your cooperation and flexibility regarding this schedule in the case of an emergency or extenuating circumstances. Any significant extra working hours will be prearranged to the extent possible and be compensated appropriately.

DUTIES AND RESPONSIBILITIES

The employee will be expected to perform the following duties:

Childcare:

- playing with the children;
- proactively planning recreational activities (e.g., play dates, arts-and-crafts projects, outings to parks/library/ pool, special events, etc.) on a weekly basis and discussing these plans in advance with the parents;
- planning, participating in and supervising at least two hours of outdoor play for the children every day (except in severe weather conditions) in addition to any other activities that may take the children out of the house. **The children must be supervised and in sight at all times when outside of our home even if they are in the backyard;**
- proactively talk to the children's teachers about school activities and how the children are doing so that we can be kept up-to-date on what is happening there;
- waking the children in the morning, dressing them, etc., in preparation for the day;
- bathing the children every evening before dinner;
- preparing and serving nutritious meals and snacks and cleaning up afterward (including putting dishes in dishwasher, washing pots, etc., running and/or emptying the dishwasher as needed, wiping up counter and table, sweeping floor [if needed], returning food and

dishes/utensils to proper place, etc.). The children are to eat all meals and snacks served at home while seated in the kitchen or at the table on the deck;

- driving the children to and from school, scheduled activities and appointments, and on outings;
- keeping children's bedrooms, playroom, and bathroom clean and organized (e.g., pick up and organize toys, make beds); putting away outdoor toys (bikes, riding toys, basketballs, etc.);
- accompanying the children to library, parties, special events, medical appointments, pool, etc., when necessary and/or if requested;
- supervising all activities in and out of the home while caring for the children (including outdoor play, play dates at our home—or out if requested to stay by child), etc.;
- appropriately disciplining the children in our absence. Good judgment and common sense work well in most situations. We prefer use of positive reinforcement and time-out with variations thereon. **Under no circumstances may physical discipline be used;**
- the children are permitted to watch up to an average total of one hour of TV or videos daily. Less is better. The only permitted TV station is PBS (Channel 13) and the only permitted videos are those we own or those that are rented of an educational and nonviolent nature (e.g., Dr. Seuss, Charlie Brown, etc.);
- responding flexibly to the needs of the children and serving as a positive role model.

Other Responsibilities:

- doing weekly grocery shopping for household and putting away the groceries;
- doing laundry for the children and parents; mending children's clothing as needed; folding and putting away the children's clothing, folding parent's clothing;

- running local errands with the children such as buying birthday gifts, dropping off/picking up dry cleaning, etc.;
- taking in mail (to be left on the kitchen counter) and taking family telephone messages;
- starting preparation of dinner in the evening including tasks such as making a salad, heating a casserole, setting the table, etc. The meals will be planned in advance in consultation with the family;
- joining in family efforts to keep the home tidy between visits from the cleaning lady.

LIVING ARRANGEMENTS

Bedroom:

Employee will have own fully furnished private bedroom on the third floor with air conditioning and own thermostat. Please do not heat or cool the room when you are not in it (i.e., working hours or if out on the weekend). *The nanny is also responsible for keeping her own room clean and organized.*

A telephone with a separate line and an answering machine will be provided for personal calls during your free time. *The nanny is responsible for paying for all calls made on this line.*

Towels and sheets will be washed on a weekly basis by the cleaning lady provided they are left by the washing machine in the morning prior to her arrival. Changing bed linens, doing personal laundry, dusting, and all other cleaning of the room is the full responsibility of the nanny.

You may entertain one friend in your room although we prefer that visits end once children are in bed due to the layout of the house; small groups of friends may be entertained in the den (see below).

Eating and drinking are not permitted in your room. *In the event that you cause any damage to the room or its contents (or elsewhere in our home), you are fully responsible for paying for the repairs.*

Kitchen and Meals:

Our kitchen is yours. We are happy to have you join us for meals or you may prepare your own, whichever you prefer. Please let us know your plans, however, so we can cook accordingly. If you wish to serve refreshments or meals to a guest(s), please let us know in advance; depending on the situation, you may be requested to purchase your supplies. Please consume all food and beverage in the kitchen.

Den/Playroom:

When the den is not being used by the children, the employee may entertain a small group (up to three) of her guests there. We ask that you let us know in advance if you would like to have guests visit.

Car:

The employee will have use of the station wagon for professional use; personal use is a privilege to be earned with safe and responsible driving and respect for the car as our property. The car will be available for personal use subject to our advance approval. You may not drive the car for long distances (more than ten miles) without our prior consent, nor may you drive into Manhattan, any of the New York boroughs, or to other highly trafficked areas (Hoboken, etc.).

You are expected to treat our car as carefully as you would your own property by driving safely at all times and keeping it clean with regular car washes and interior vacuuming. We will pay for gas as it relates to professional use and for regular maintenance; in cases when personal use has resulted in excessive wear and tear or gas consumption, you are responsible for these costs. If the employee receives a ticket or has an accident in which she is at fault, she is responsible for paying any costs incurred as a result. **Under no circumstances whatsoever will unsafe driving or drinking and driving be tolerated.**

SALARY AND BENEFITS

The employee will be paid $XXX every Friday after completing the work week. You may receive up to $XXX as an educational stipend for classes that we mutually agree are related to job responsibilities. This will be paid when you complete the class with a passing grade.

There are ten vacation/personal days. We require that the employee coordinate *all* vacation plans with those of our family. No vacation may be taken in the first four months of employment unless it is to coordinate with our vacation. From time to time, the employee will be invited to join our family on vacation. If you work during this vacation, the compensation arrangement shall be negotiated and agreed upon before the holiday commences.

There are six legal paid holidays: New Year's Day, President's Day, Memorial Day, July 4th, Thanksgiving Day, and Christmas Day. We will be inviting you to join us in celebrating some of the major holidays with our family and hope that you will join us.

HOUSE RULES

We expect the employee to come home at a respectable hour in the evening so as to not interfere with job-related duties the next day. On the weekends or holidays, if you expect to be out very late or not return that evening, kindly let us know in advance so we do not worry needlessly.

Friends may visit with our prior approval. We ask that the employee not have a guest in her own room once any family member is getting ready for bed and also that she limit herself to one guest in the room at a time (unless this is discussed with and agreed to by us in advance). We prefer that the employee not entertain a male guest in her room. Overnight guests are not allowed without our prior approval.

We respect each others' privacy and rights. Simple courtesies, such as knocking and waiting for a reply before opening a door, emptying the dishwasher or kitchen garbage, keeping the common rooms tidy and cleaning up after oneself, are practiced and appreciated in our home. We also ask that you respect our family's privacy by not discussing with your own friends or family any personal matters that may arise in our private lives.

All food and beverages are to be consumed in the kitchen or on the deck.

Smoking is not permitted in our home or car by anyone, guests or resident.

Personal telephone calls may not be made or accepted while on duty except in an emergency.

TERMINATION OF AGREEMENT

This agreement may be terminated by either party by providing four weeks' notice to the other. Recession can take place in a lesser period by mutual consent or if the terms of this contract are violated. This agreement may be amended by mutual consent only.

The undersigned agree to the terms, duties, and schedule as described above.

Employee   Date

Employer   Date

MAKING THE OFFER FOR IN-HOME CHILDCARE

Chances are that you are delighted to have found the best-qualified candidate to care for your children. Make sure that this sentiment is conveyed to the candidate when you make an offer. For in-home childcare, you should already have a good idea if the candidate would accept your offer (and sign the contract, of course) if it is extended. With that in mind, you decide if you want to make the offer personally or, if you have used an agency, have the agency do it. When you make the offer, convey your pleasure to have found a person who is so well qualified and who the children like, quickly review the Job Requirements, and determine the start date. We gave our nanny the written agreement toward the end of her face-to-face interview (she had flown in from the Midwest to spend a weekend with our family). We told her to think about it overnight although we were delighted when she accepted on the spot and signed.

ENROLLING YOUR CHILD IN A FAMILY DAY CARE OR DAY-CARE CENTER

For day care (family or center-based), you will need to confirm the process of enrolling your child with the director.

At that time, reaffirm that the caregiver who you have interviewed and observed will be working with your child because center staffing and assignments can sometimes change. In the event that the best childcare center has a long waiting list, consider using an interim childcare arrangement if at all possible.

Be prepared for a lot of paperwork to read and sign. You will also need to provide medical records, doctor contacts, and insurance information if it is a licensed day-care center. Carefully review all the Rules and Requirements and ask any last-minute questions before you actually write your first check. For family day care, make sure that you and the caregiver both know and understand the basic ground rules to prevent any conflicts or misunderstandings in the future.

MEDICAL EMERGENCY LETTER

Give your caregiver at least two copies of a Medical Emergency Letter along with a copy of your insurance card. She should carry the letter with her at all times. (Note: Most day-care centers require this when you enroll and provide their own form for you to complete.) The letter should authorize the caregiver (by name) to allow emergency medical services in the event that your child requires them and you or your spouse (or other specified family members or close friends) cannot be reached for consent. Put phone numbers of all these contact people as well as your doctors in the letter.

While no parent wants to think about emergencies happening to their child while she is apart from you, you must be prepared for dealing with this contingency. If you do not have enough confidence in the caregiver's common sense to give her this letter, think about why you are comfortable allowing her to watch your child at all. A copy of our letter's format is below.

SAMPLE MEDICAL EMERGENCY LETTER

Caregiver should carry one copy in purse and have one in the house. If letter is more than one page long, STAPLE all the pages together.

Your address
Re: List all your children by full name

To Whom It May Concern:
   CAREGIVER NAME has my permission to authorize appropriate emergency medical treatment for my children, CHILD NAME and CHILD NAME, in the event that my husband or I or any other authorized emergency contacts (below) cannot be reached in a timely manner.
   Our pediatrician is Dr. ABC (PHONE and ADDRESS) and our dentist is Dr. XYZ (PHONE and ADDRESS). CHILD NAME has the following medical conditions you should note: (include and complete if applicable with all necessary details).
   I accept financial responsibility for any such emergency treatment. Below is my insurance information.

Sincerely,
YOUR SIGNATURE
Print your name

Emergency contacts
Your name: work and home phone number
Spouse name: work and home phone number
Other names: work and home phone number (Put one or two, such as a grandparent or best friend.)

Insurance info
(Photocopy of your card or note name of insurer, telephone number, policy number, etc.)

• • •

In closing your search, all I have to add is: *Congratulations, you did it!*

By now, you have probably realized that your search for quality childcare is an important step in the process of raising a happy, healthy child. Your goal was to find the quality childcare your child deserves so that he can be happy, loved, and secure while you are at work. A key variable in this equation is to ensure that the childcare arrangement and/or caregiver establishes a long-standing and stable relationship with both you and your child. The next chapter will offer you some ideas on how to achieve this vital objective.

PART III

Keeping Quality Childcare

Tips to Make It Work

FINDING AND HIRING high-quality childcare is a long process, but it is just the beginning. Most parents hope to develop a long-term relationship with the selected childcare provider and arrangement. There are many solid reasons behind this desire. First, stability in childcare arrangements is good for your children; it helps them to feel secure in a positive relationship with a caring adult in a caring environment. Second, stability in childcare arrangements is good for you; the search process itself is tough, and who wants to do that again soon? This chapter will offer some tips on how to make your childcare arrangement an ongoing success.

HOW DO I KNOW MY CHILD IS RECEIVING QUALITY CHILDCARE?

The question of what goes on during your child's day while you are working is one that haunts most working parents.

How do you know that your child is being treated with love and that her needs are being attended to? It is particularly difficult to answer these concerns if you have an infant or young child, who cannot speak.

When trying to assess the quality of the childcare, you need to tread a fine line. Your efforts can easily be interpreted as meddling, nosy, or distrustful, all of which can eventually alienate or offend even a wonderful caregiver. Be sensitive to this possibility and act accordingly but *never abdicate and always exercise your right to know what is going on with your child while you are not with her.*

There are several ways in which you can ascertain the quality of the childcare, all of which are based upon your conscientious efforts to observe and communicate. The importance of observing and communicating may be obvious, but in the rush of daily working life, you will often need to remind yourself to do so. Here are some hints to get you started:

1. *Solicit feedback from your child*

Even the youngest of infants can communicate, if only by body language and behavior. Does the child seem to be in a foul mood on the days when he is in childcare or is he content? How does he respond to the caregiver when he arrives at childcare, when he is leaving, when he is being held by her? Does your child maintain eye contact with the caregiver, you, and others? Is he animated with you, indicating that he expects to and does interact with others during the day? Does he have a chronic case of weekday diaper rash that clears up when you are with him on the weekend? Are the diapers you supply being used at the rate that you expect or use on the days you are home?

For young children who are speaking and mobile (crawling, chattering), are they developing these skills at the appropriate pace, demonstrating a stimulating age-appropriate environment? What are their words and actions telling you about their activities and enjoyment of the day in childcare?

Listen to any off-hand comments your child may make; they can be very revealing. One neighbor had a problem with her three-year-old jumping off the kitchen table and counters; even time-out punishments did not halt the behavior. Finally, she asked the child why she was persisting with such unacceptable behavior. The child replied with clear exasperation "But (caregiver) lets me do this all the time at her house!" My neighbor followed up by asking the caregiver about this (always do a reality check), found out that it was true, and by expressing her concern, worked with the caregiver to resolve the problem.

What child feedback really boils downs to is that you know your child, you are attuned to her "signals," and your gut feeling about how she feels about the childcare arrangement and caregiver is probably on target. When Sam was an infant in family day care, I was able to tell he was receiving quality care by his degree of comfort when he was held by the caregiver and by seeing that he consistently had so much fun playing with and watching the other children that he would not notice I had arrived to pick him up.

It is important to understand that developmental delays are not always a sign of poor-quality care. You may even find that an experienced and dedicated caregiver will express concerns about developmental delays in your child before you notice them—especially if it is your firstborn. My younger son has a severe speech delay. I knew better than to blame our nanny for this problem.

2. *Solicit feedback from your neighbors, other parents in the childcare arrangement*

If you have in-home care, let your neighbors know that

the caregiver will be there. Indicate that you welcome having their eyes watching while you are away from your child. Casually inquire if they see the nanny and children outdoors on nice days, if the nanny plays with the children or just watches them play. You may also get feedback from merchants in town, the pediatrician, and others (if you have the caregiver do these activities with your child). Try to gauge the enthusiasm of the feedback. If someone seems reluctant to say anything, it may mean that it is not good news or that the person is just reticent. Be open to unsolicited feedback and glean information from it. For example Sam broke his arm in preschool and neither my husband nor I could be reached. Without instruction, our nanny brought him to the doctor and then the orthopedist. (This is a very good example of why you need a Medical Emergency Letter.) Several parents at the school, the pediatrician, and the orthopedist volunteered comments on how well she handled the emergency and how much the children seemed to love her. Whenever I have a casual chat with a neighbor and mention our nanny, they always note how much the children love her and how they are always outdoors playing.

For center-based care, make a concerted effort to connect with other parents during pickup, drop-off, or family activities to learn of their own observations and impressions as well as any concerns they may have. Even a brief chat during the short walk down the hall can provide you with new insights. Talk to other caregivers and staff members because you may learn about developments at the center before they are announced (e.g., there is a state exam expected, "Ms. Smith" is pregnant, etc.).

3. *Drop in during the day*

Leave your job early or during lunch and drop in unannounced to see what your child is doing (either at home or at the center). Do this irregularly but with some frequency. Call your home or the center occasionally to find out what everyone is up to. This is one of the best ways to get an unedited view of what is really going on.

4. *Always communicate with the caregiver and be attuned to the environment*

Talk to the caregiver and see if, without your prompting, she observes the same things about your child that you do. Ask what happened during the day and see if it is consistent with what you expected to be happening and what your child is "telling" you. If you have a concern about your child, raise it with the caregiver to get her feedback.

A former colleague came home to find a cigarette butt in the powder room toilet of her nonsmoking home. When she asked the nanny about it, the nanny said it was hers. Because smoking was not permitted in the home and the nanny initially claimed she did not smoke, it meant that either she was lying about her own habit when directly asked or that she had a guest over during the day, which was not permitted. This incident marked the start of a period when the mother lost confidence in the nanny's credibility and integrity. This confidence was not regained, and eventually the nanny was dismissed.

Finally, and quite importantly, if you have any *real* suspicion that your child is being emotionally or physically abused (however you may define that term), terminate the childcare relationship *immediately* and, if you feel it is warranted, report the matter to the authorities. You can worry about your childcare arrangement *after* you have secured the safety of your child!

WHAT IF I MADE A MISTAKE?

The flip side to confirming that your child is indeed getting quality childcare or that your child loves a truly wonderful caregiver is the discovery that despite all your hard work and effort, you may have made a mistake in your choice of caregiver or childcare arrangement. Unfortunately, this can happen too.

If you believe that your child is in a *totally* unacceptable situation, terminate the arrangement *immediately*. In all other cases (e.g., the caregiver or arrangement is just not meeting your needs as you had hoped), take the time to analyze the situation carefully before you act. Identify the source of your discomfort or dissatisfaction so that you can try to work with the caregiver to alleviate it, or if not, at least avoid repeating the same mistake for your next childcare choice. For example, are you using a live-in caregiver and finding that your family lifestyle and home just cannot accommodate another adult? Or did you think that the Happy Days Center was perfect only to find that your child does not thrive in a structured environment? Many times, problems arise only after you are actually in the situation and test how it really works. Sometimes, however, you recognize that the misgivings (gut feelings) you may have had when making compromises or checking references were indeed valid and should not have been disregarded. *In all instances, you can and must learn from your mistakes and move on.*

Center-based care may have notification requirements and charges when you withdraw your child early; check the rules and requirements to determine what these are. Work within the terms of your contract and give notice accordingly. If you used an agency that has a replacement policy, let them know that you will need a new caregiver and find out what the process is, especially in terms of timing. Ideally, you have a professional and civil relationship with the nanny; be honest and give her a few weeks' notice. This should give you enough time to plan a smooth transition while you seek another childcare arrangement or caregiver. Consider offering a severance package to your nanny if you can afford to (payable in full on the predetermined last day of employment) to induce the caregiver to stay until you have made alternative arrangements.

If the arrangement is not working out, don't be surprised if the caregiver beats you to the punch and quits either before you terminate her or before your agreed end date. To prevent being totally surprised and unprepared, give some prior thought to Plan B: "What Will I Do Until I Find a New Childcare Arrangement?" You may have had a second choice when you made the initial hiring decision. See if this is an option you wish to pursue seriously (after all, it was your *second* choice) and if so, find out if the person or center is still available. Investigate if there are any agencies that place temporary childcare providers or day-care centers that permit short-term childcare place-ments. Talk to friends and relatives about lending a hand and count up any vacation days that you and your spouse may have. Whatever you do, do not give in to despair or make any decisions out of desperation; if you do so, you will find yourself reading this section again in short order!

BEING A GOOD MANAGER

A few weeks after I returned to work following Sam's birth, it occurred to me that I was the "manager" in the childcare relationship. Of course, I had hired and paid people before to do things around my house or for other services, but never before had I had a long-term, paying relationship with someone I had trusted with *so much* re-sponsibility. This was something new. I realized that the nature of my relationship with the caregiver was almost as important as my child's relationship with her.

As a working parent, you already know what it feels like to be an employee and how important it is to your job satisfaction to have a good working relationship with your boss. In some cases, you may also have had practice being a manager and perhaps understand what fosters good and bad employee relations. While the childcare situation is not exactly analogous to your own work situation, the key considerations of respect, compensation, and communication are applicable to both in ensuring a positive and successful working relationship.

Respect

Respect consists of two elements: the overall relationship of mutual respect between the manager and employee as individuals *and* as professionals, and the respect of the manager for the employee's ability to meet the demands of the job and for the quality of the work performed.

Respect for the caregiver is conveyed by your words *and* your actions. Always make the effort to ask how the day went with your child, and then listen carefully to the answer. If it was a tough day (e.g., baby teething, toddler cranky), recognize it as such and commend the caregiver for successfully coping. Make an effort to ask the caregiver for her opinions on how to deal with childrearing issues you may be facing (such as separation anxiety, sleep problems, toilet training, etc.). Acknowledge and thank the caregiver if you know that she is making an extraordinary effort in helping you with a childcare matter. (Both my children were toilet trained primarily by their caregivers, for which I am *eternally* grateful.) Positive feedback from your praise and appreciation can make a big impact.

It is also important that your *actions* demonstrate respect. If you fail to honor the terms of the contract (or the rules of the center), do not expect the caregiver always to live by these terms in return. For example, if your nanny is supposed to work until 6:00 P.M. and you must work late, call to let her know and pay her for working overtime; don't take her for granted. If the center has a 6:00 P.M. pickup time, call ahead if you know you will be late and always apologize once you arrive (as you pay your late fine). Finally, never underestimate the significance of a token gift, such as flowers, candy, a card, or a scarf, to commemorate a big event (e.g., toilet training, contract renewal, etc.), holidays, and birthdays. These gestures can convey your thanks when you may have been lax about otherwise expressing it.

Keep in mind that the caregiver is not you, so not everything will be done in the exact same way that you might do it. Be open-minded about these differences; not each one is worth raising as an issue or arguing over. You may learn of a better way to do something in the process, especially if you are a new parent. You have hired this person for the job because you trust her with the responsibility of caring for your child; be prepared to allow the caregiver the latitude to do her job well.

Finally, although you ought to maintain some professional distance so that your expectations and the job responsibilities remain the primary focus of your relationship with the caregiver, recognize that she is an individual with her own life and problems. (Are you best friends with your manager? Probably not. But you would probably tell her of a death in your family if it were affecting your work. These things can happen to caregivers too.)

Compensation

There are many factors that contribute to the satisfaction one derives from a job. Intangibles such as feeling respected and appreciated are crucial. But receiving fair compensation—both salary and other benefits—is a vital component that tangibly communicates the value of the work. If you had a job in which you felt underpaid, it would be difficult for you to remain satisfied, or loyal, in the long term. Making the childcare position rewarding to the caregiver requires your concerted efforts and involves fair compensation, and regular benefit reviews and/or increases, along with the other points noted herein.

Communication

Communication consists of three important elements: regular give-and-take with the caregiver; clear mutual understanding of the job requirements and performance standards; and constructive criticism along with positive reinforcement on caregiver performance.

You know how hard it is to do a good job if you lack a clear idea of what needs to be done. The same applies in a childcare relationship. Before you hold the caregiver to specific performance standards or job requirements, make certain that they have been expressed and understood. This is one of the best reasons for having a contract.

Encourage the caregiver to ask you any questions or express any concerns that may arise regarding your child. Also, tell her of any issues in your private life that may be affecting your child (grandparent illness, night terrors, etc.). Make sure that you recognize a job well done, both verbally and by your actions. If there is a problem, be forthright in raising the matter with the caregiver and fair-minded as you formulate and implement the solution. The next section of this chapter has some concrete suggestions for ways in which you can enhance communication with the caregiver.

In sum, your managerial goal is to establish a parenting partnership with the caregiver such that this is not just a paycheck but also an emotionally rewarding job for her. Nonetheless, keep in mind that you are the manager, and even in a partnership there is the senior partner. This is not a democracy where everyone's vote has equal weight. A quality caregiver can offer a great deal of insight and useful advice regarding childcare matters; whenever possible these ideas should be taken into account and given your serious consideration. However, it is still your child and it remains your decision as to how *major* issues should be handled. If you have insurmountable differences with the caregiver on an issue that is of great importance to both of you, you have two alternatives: work out a solution with which you can both abide or consider changing to a new caregiver.

COMMUNICATION IDEAS

Clearly, one of the keys to your successful caregiver relationship, as well as to your determination that your child is getting quality care, is using communication as a tool to know what is going on with your child while you are at work. Here are some specific suggestions for making this happen.

1. *Daily Update*
   When the childcare day ends, remember to ask the caregiver how it went, what she and your child did, and what is planned for the next day. Listen to the answers and ask questions. Some day-care centers and caregivers also keep a written log of each day's activities. Bring up issues about which you may be concerned. ("Is Adam drinking enough milk?" "Does he seem even vaguely interested in toilet training?" "What was his mood like—he slept poorly last night?") Brainstorm with the caregiver on solutions to problems or on activity ideas ("He really loves to color. What kind of activities do you think he would enjoy for this?" "Any ideas on how we can promote this 'potty' concept to him?" "I am worried that he may be starting to bite when he is angry. How can we deal this?").

2. *Weekly Schedule*
   Traditional day-care centers and some family-based centers often have predetermined daily schedules. For other family day care and in most in-home childcare arrangements, the

structure of the day and the schedule is more relaxed. When we used family day care, the caregiver and I would discuss major events and excursions planned for the next few days (e.g., a trip to visit her parents and play in their yard, swimming sessions at the municipal pool, etc.). With in-home care, I used a written weekly schedule that was discussed with the nanny at the start of the week and posted on the refrigerator. This was partly because my children developed very busy social lives (for young children, that is) and also because we wanted to ensure that they got to do certain activities and that certain chores or errands were done. The schedule provided all of us with a point of reference as well as useful reminders once the work week got hectic.

3. *Scheduled Conferences*

This may sound somewhat daunting but I encourage you to consider scheduling periodic conferences with the caregiver; these are somewhat comparable to a parent-teacher conference once your child is in school. The purpose of the conference is to focus your collective thinking on the bigger issues: "Is the child doing well with this arrangement?" "Is the caregiver satisfied with the job?" "What problems or concerns does she have?" "Am I satisfied with the caregiver?" "What problems or concerns do I have?" "How can we resolve some of the issues that may have been raised here?" It is an opportunity for everyone to sit down and air any issues that may have been neglected in the day-to-day rush and to give constructive feedback, both positive and negative. Try to have these conferences at least twice a year and plan on spending about a half hour for each one. Some day-care centers schedule these as part of their normal operation; if not, or if you are not using a day-care center, schedule them at your own initiative.

I cannot overemphasize the importance of establishing strong and ongoing communication with the caregiver. This person is your window into your child's world while you are away from her. Communication is an important tool in keeping this window open.

SOMEONE NEW IS LIVING WITH US: MAINTAINING SMOOTH RELATIONS WITH A LIVE-IN NANNY

Having a nanny live in your home brings the childcare manager-employee relationship to a different plane. Imagine what you would feel like if you lived with your manager. Try to treat the live-in nanny as you would hope to be treated in the same situation. Unless you have a very large home or one with a separate entrance to the nanny's living quarters, it is hard to ignore the fact that there is someone living in your house who is intimately involved with a very important aspect of your lives yet is not a family member.

If you have chosen to hire a very young person to be the caregiver (e.g., an eighteen-year-old au pair who is far from home), you must think about the concept of being "in loco parentis." Like it or not, when you commit to this type of childcare arrangement, as a responsible adult you are buying in to this role, regardless of what the placement agency may tell you. From time to time, the young person in your home may need your mature guidance as a proxy for a trusted older friend. In doing this, however, avoid becoming overly involved in the tribulations of young adulthood. You are *not* her parent and you do not have the same responsibilities toward her as her parents do—don't give yourself an ulcer worrying about her personal problems. Remember to keep your perspective and try to view the experience as a trial run for when your own children reach this age.

Privacy for the Caregiver—Physical and Emotional

When the workday ends for your caregiver, respect her privacy and time alone. Her bedroom is the only private space she has in your home and your family should not enter unless invited. (Obviously, if you think that something is *seriously* amiss, you should enter under any circumstance.) When her door is closed and she is off duty, do not disturb her unless it is very important. Teach your children the concept of private time for the nanny so they do not pester her. Avoid the strong temptation to knock on her door and ask for a series of small favors during this private time (e.g., "Can you watch the kids for ten minutes while I run to the supermarket?"). Frequent yet minor intrusions such as these can snowball into big resentments. If the nanny wants to be with you and your family, she will communicate this in her actions.

Avoid the temptation to become overly involved in your caregiver's personal life and problems. You have hired someone to be a caregiver for your child, not your best friend. (This does not preclude you from being sympathetic or offering advice when solicited.) While it is clearly important for you to be aware of personal issues that may impact the nanny's job performance (and that you may try to help her resolve), your primary role is that of the manager and your chief concern is the welfare of your child.

Family Life and Your Own Privacy

On the other hand, you and your family might also want some private time as a family. Establish some parameters up front so that the nanny feels welcome to join in family activities at mutually comfortable times. For example, you may have a weekly family TGIF pizza dinner or video night when you try to reconnect with your children after a long work week, and plan fun activities for the weekend. This may be something that you feel is just for your family. Be kind but straightforward in explaining to the nanny your feelings about this evening if she seems upset by not being included. The nanny should be welcome to use your kitchen and join the family for most regular meals if she wishes (after all, she may need to eat at roughly the same times). If there is a big holiday celebration (Thanksgiving, July 4th, Christmas) and your nanny is far from her own relatives, invite her to join your family. It would be highly insensitive (and cruel) not to do so. This also includes inviting her to your child's birthday parties. There is the possibility that she may choose not to join you for some or any of these events (don't be offended, this is her free time), but the invitations should be sincerely extended.

House Rules

In your home, there are most likely a set of unwritten house rules that everyone somehow knows and abides by, such as no smoking, taking off shoes when you come through the front door, or clearing dishes and loading the dishwasher right after eating. Because the live-in nanny is a newcomer to your home, you need to recognize that she does not know these things. For those house rules that are extremely important to you and your family, be thoughtful enough to explain them up front. We have a section on house rules in our nanny contract. Nonetheless, do not set up an extensive system of special restrictive rules that apply only to the nanny because this can foster ill will and can be really quite unfair.

CAN I BE FRIENDS WITH THE CAREGIVER? SETTING THE TONE OF YOUR RELATIONSHIP

Remember: *You have hired someone to be a caregiver for your child, not to be your friend.* I believe that in order for the childcare arrangement to succeed, you must recognize and understand this central fact: *This is a WORKING relationship.* Just as you can have a cordial relationship with your manager but most likely try to keep some professional distance, you should seek to do the same in this relationship as well. Of course, the tone of your relationship with the caregiver will vary according to the person and the type of arrangement you have chosen, but this idea of not mixing friendship and business should stand. (Generally, it is easier to maintain a professional distance when you have out-of-home childcare.)

There is a very big difference between "being friends" and "being friendly." It seems as if I am suggesting that you cannot have a true *friendship* with the caregiver, and I suppose that I am. The childcare arrangement and the parent-caregiver relationship is not fundamentally democratic in nature. Your objective should be to establish a *friendly* relationship with the caregiver that is based upon mutual respect and a genuine fondness for each other. While you and the caregiver are partners in sharing the same goal (namely the well-being of your child), one of you must be there to guide. As the parent and the manager, it is your responsibility to fill this role. Moreover, there will be times when you and the caregiver have differences of opinion on matters of importance relating to your child. When you feel strongly enough to take a stand on such an issue, you need to be the manager in order to solve the matter. Being good friends with the caregiver may limit your ability to give directions and criticism *effectively*. Moreover, it can sometimes cloud your judgment or influence your actions when you are assessing whether the arrangement or caregiver is meeting your childcare needs and requirements.

Although this advice may sound coldhearted, in practice it is not. While the fundamentals differ, this is loosely analogous to the parent-child relationship, which is also not a democracy. With your child (who you undoubtedly love), you must be the parent first and foremost, with the respect and authority that accompany that role. Your child's friends play a very different role in your child's life. In the parent-caregiver relationship, you must be the manager first and foremost.

HELP, I THINK MY CHILD LOVES THE CAREGIVER MORE THAN ME: DEALING WITH YOUR JEALOUSY

This book ends with advice on a problem that I hope and pray will be the worst one you encounter with quality childcare: you become jealous—maybe even *really* jealous. If you have been successful in your search for quality childcare, the day will come when you finish a tough day at work with high hopes for a pleasant evening of family time, and instead your child starts to cry at the sight of you because he does not want to leave the caregiver.

Your first thought is, "What did I do wrong?" followed by "He loves *her* more than he loves me!" then "I think I'm going to cry too!" and finally, "I hate that woman! She's fired!"

Stop. Take a deep breath and think about it. You have devoted an incredible amount of time and energy to find the best caregiver and childcare arrangement possible for your child. You have worked hard to foster a relationship of mutual respect and trust. You wanted a caregiver and childcare arrangement that makes your child feel secure, loved, and happy. Your child's tears are evidence of what you wanted all along: *Your child loves his caregiver! This is* good—*in fact, this is* great*! You are witnessing a demonstration of your success!* How can you be upset in knowing that you have succeeded in finding quality childcare for your child?

Rest assured that love is not a limited resource. Your child can and should love a lot of people besides you. In fact, the more, the better. Loving the caregiver does not mean that your child stops loving you. I have heard stories of parents who have fired caregivers because their children have become "too close" to them, or who only hire au pairs with one-year visas so that their children do not develop too close a relationship. I cannot fathom this sentiment.

This book may contain some strong advice but this is the only absolute dictate you will find herein: You are a parent and you are an adult. Under no circumstances should you allow your jealousy of a healthy love that your child has for a quality caregiver or that the caregiver has for your child to cause you to sever that bond.

SOME THOUGHTS IN CLOSING

The overriding message to derive from this book is that you *can* find and keep quality childcare without losing your mind. A working parent who systematically and rationally approaches the search for quality childcare can be successful by practicing the following:

- Be prepared by understanding the various elements of your childcare needs and your available options in filling them;
- Be knowledgeable on how to conduct your search effectively by identifying and using productive search resources;
- Be comfortable, perceptive, and thorough as you screen, interview, and check references;
- Be a fair and conscientious manager.

Compromise when and where needed. But the bottom line is that as long as you have realistic and appropriate requirements for a childcare arrangement and caregiver, stick to your guns. Your choice of a childcare arrangement and caregiver is extremely important to the well-being of your child. Your standards *should* be high! In this life, you cannot choose your parents, but you can choose your spouse. You cannot choose your children but you can choose their caregiver and arrangement.

Good luck—you truly have my best wishes for success. May you find the quality childcare that both you and your child deserve.

Appendices

Parenting Philosophy

- Childhood should be fun.
- Children should be secure in knowing that they are un-conditionally loved.
- Say yes whenever possible. When you say no, make sure you mean it.
- Choose your battles carefully . . . not everything is worth a fight. Avoid winning the battle but losing the war.
- Admit when you are wrong, and apologize.
- No physical discipline.
- You are the adult and you are in charge; ultimately the children know this so you don't have to prove it.
- Children are like sponges; they hear and see everything so be careful of what you say or do even when you think they are not watching.
- Always remember that you are a role model.
- Treat the child with the same respect you would want to receive.
- Obedience can be demanded; respect must be earned. As a parent, I would rather be respected.
- You cannot "control" a child. You *can* influence a situation, guide behavior, elicit cooperation, and suggest a path.
- Encourage independence and creativity.
- Praise the child for doing good things; positive reinforcement is the best form of discipline.
- Build the child's self-esteem and self-confidence.
- It is more important to try your best than to succeed.
- Getting dirty is okay—it all comes off in the wash.

Sample Marketing Package
Nanny Position

Employer: Michelle Ehrich and Andrew Ross
Address and Phone

Children: Sam Ross (born July 1990)
Adam Ross (born January 1993)

Family Description:

(Note to the reader: This is a big part of our "selling" the job.)

The primary focus in our lives is our family. When we have free time, we seek to spend it with the children, usually just hanging out and playing. It is very important to us that we try to have a family dinner every night (however simple the meal) and that we put the kids to bed with a bath and story. Since we do spend a large part of our day at work, we want to ensure that our free time is well spent and, to us, that means with our kids.

Sam is a very good-natured and bright preschooler. He has a good vocabulary and excellent reasoning skills. In addition, he is quite tall and physically dexterous for his age. He is also very shy around strangers and in new situations (even if he knows everyone there), especially if his mom or dad is around to keep him company. In that respect, we've been told he takes after both his parents as children.

Adam is a very happy and laid-back toddler with a sweet disposition. He goes with the flow although he does love to sit on our laps and is a real climber. He has also demonstrated more of a mischievous streak than his brother had at the same age. The boys get along well and are starting to play together nicely although there is still some sibling rivalry to overcome.

Michelle grew up in a small town in New Jersey and Andrew comes from a small town in Upstate New York. We both work in Manhattan at banks.

Our family is Jewish and we observe the major religious holidays. We are not Orthodox in our beliefs, which means that we do not go to temple every week, nor do we follow a special diet. We have a wide range of friends of all religions.

Position Description:

(Note to the reader: This is taken directly from our Job Description.)

1. Primary Responsibility: The children are your first and most important responsibility, everything else (e.g., laundry, dishes, etc.) is secondary. They need to be played with, read to, cared for while we are at work. We are looking for someone who will actively interact with our children and not just watch them. We hope that you will be a positive role model for our children, teaching them kindness, confidence, responsibility, and consideration.

2. General Duties revolve around caring for our children while we are at work:

- Get children up and dressed in the morning; bathe them before we get home for dinner.
- Prepare children's breakfast and lunch and start family dinner; clean up kitchen after breakfast and lunch. On infrequent occasions when we have an evening engagement, you may be asked to prepare the children's dinner and clean up.

- Keep children's bedrooms and playroom neat. Do children's laundry, mending, etc.
- Drive children to preschool and other daytime activities and appointments (pediatrician, etc.).
- Entertain children during the day with activities at home and in the yard, and with trips to park, library, shops in town, etc.
- Do a limited amount of local errands with children if time permits (including the grocery shopping with Adam when Sam is in school).

3. Days and hours: We usually leave for work by 6:20 A.M. and return by 6:00 P.M. You are on duty when we are out of the house, even if the children are still asleep. You will be working from Monday morning through Friday evening with weekday evenings free. You will be off from Friday evening until Monday morning.

4. Tenure: We are seeking someone who, upon finding an enjoyable childcare position, is interested in staying for at least eighteen to twenty-four months.

Candidate Qualifications:

(Note to the reader: This is taken directly from our Candidate Qualifications.)

- Genuine love and appreciation of children and desire to care for them.
- Prior childcare experience. Childcare training (e.g., nanny certificate) is a welcome credential.
- Good judgment and common sense.
- Energetic and enjoys playing with children.
- Well spoken.
- Creative.
- No smoking. No drug use or alcohol abuse, past or present

- Good health and grooming.
- Three work references (at least two childcare); two personal references (nonfamily); family references (we will want to speak with your parents and/or children).
- Clean driving record (and valid driver's license) and no police record. Experience in heavy suburban driving is a plus.
- High school graduate and some college or nanny courses
- Some first aid knowledge.
- Basic cooking skills.
- Lived away from home for at least three months.

(Note to the reader: The next two sections comprise the compensation and benefits that we considered when we formulated the Job Description/Requirements.)

Amenities and Accommodations:

Private bedroom: New bed and furniture, TV, clock radio, phone with separate line and answering machine. You are responsible for all toll calls on this line.

Shared bathroom with the children: This is a very large and renovated hall bathroom, which also houses the washer and dryer. There is plenty of cabinet space for storage of personal items. Since the children are so young, with the exception of bath time in the evenings, they spend little time using this room.

Playroom/den: We have a large, newly finished playroom, which is carpeted and furnished. When the toys are put away, it serves as a den. You may use this room to entertain friends when you are off duty provided the children are not using it.

Car: We have two cars. During the week, one will be available to you to transport the children or if you go out at night. On the weekend, you may have personal use of the car *most of the time and with our agreement.* You are expected to drive carefully and to pay for any damage you may cause to the car or tickets you receive.

Compensation:

Salary: To be determined. A raise will be considered annually.
Vacation: Two weeks (ten working days) plus two days at Christmas. If you are asked to accompany us on vacation to work, compensation will be prearranged. We do ask that you coordinate your vacation plans with ours. In addition, we recommend (although it is certainly not a requirement) that you plan to take some extra time off around the Christmas holiday.
Holidays: There are a total of six holidays—New Year's Day, President's Day, Memorial Day, July 4th, Thanksgiving Day, and Christmas Day.

Community and Neighborhood:

(Note to the reader: This is a big part of our "selling" the job.)

Westfield is truly a lovely town with a great sense of civic pride. The town, located in the suburban New York City area, has a population of about thirty thousand and is two hundred years old. Most of the streets are tree lined and there is a mix of Victorian, colonial, and newer homes. Among the activities in town are a local symphony, a community theater and orchestra, a community pool, YMCA, an arts workshop and recreation programs, various recreational clubs, several churches of virtually all denominations, several town parks with playgrounds, lakes, tennis, soccer, baseball, and basketball facilities, and a newly expanded public library. Westfield is well known for an excellent school system that also offers a wonderful adult school with night classes on a tremendous variety of subjects. There is also a large downtown with two movie theaters (five screens), dozens of restaurants (Chinese, Italian, French, Japanese, American, etc.), over a hundred shops, and a large upscale department store. Westfield has train and bus lines into New York City; it is about a forty-five minute ride and many residents commute to jobs in New York or go in to enjoy the cultural attractions there. In addition, the town is about thirty miles from the Jersey beaches on the Atlantic, among the nicest in the Northeast.

Our neighborhood is unique in that it is a quiet area yet just a short walk to downtown, the train, and the bus. The homes are older and well maintained. Our neighbors are very friendly (there is a summer block party and a holiday party in the winter) and there are lots of kids.

(Note to the reader: We included photos of both boys and of our home in springtime when the dogwood tree was in bloom.)

Sample Nanny School Letter

Your Address

Professional Nanny Program
XYZ University
City, State ZIP

Attention: Carol Jones, Assistant Professor

Dear Ms. Jones,

Thank you for the explanatory letter outlining the nanny program at XYZ University and your job-posting procedures. Enclosed you will find a job description for a nanny position we are seeking to fill. The attached is quite detailed but in sum, my husband and I are seeking an energetic, responsible, and cheerful person to live in our home in a suburb of New York City and care for our two young boys while we are at work. We believe that we offer an attractive compensation package as well as a pleasant working and living environment. We are interested in hiring an individual to start in the springtime (or summer).

I would be grateful if you could put the enclosed job description in any placement book or postings that your office maintains and perhaps advise any qualified individuals who are interested in relocating to this area of our open position. Please encourage any prospective candidates who would like to learn more about this job to contact me directly at my office (212–111–2222 from 8:00 A.M. until 4:00 P.M.) or home (908–333–4444 before 9:00 P.M.) or by mail at our home. In addition, I look forward to receiving your graduates list in February.

Thank you for your help.

Sincerely,
YOUR SIGNATURE

Sample Direct Recruitment Letter

Dear Kim,

We recently received your name on the list of May graduates of the XYZ University professional nanny program. (Please excuse this form letter but we wanted to contact all prospective candidates as quickly as we could.) We were hoping that you would be interested in considering the nanny position that our family is offering. We have two young sons (Sam, three and a half years, and Adam, one year) both of whom are active and sweet natured; we live in Westfield, New Jersey, which is close enough to New York City to enjoy its pleasures yet far enough to escape its hassles.

Option A: In January, we sent a very detailed family and job description along with photos to Janet Smith for inclusion in the university's placement program (please note that it may be filed under my name or my husband's name, Andrew Ross).

Option B: Enclosed is a description of the position we are offering as well as of our community. We encourage you to look at our profile to see if you would like to apply for our job. If you decide you are interested, please drop us a short letter telling us a bit about yourself, your childcare experience, why you are interested in applying for our position, and anything else you may want us to know. We will call you upon receipt of your letter to set up a telephone interview.

Although we realize that you are not available until May, we would like to finish interviewing candidates by sometime in March (with the understanding that there will be a delayed start date), so we do ask you to let us know very soon if would like to apply to be a nanny with our family. We hope to receive your letter and have the opportunity to speak with you soon.

Sincerely yours,
YOUR SIGNATURE

Sample Interview Questions—In-Home and Center Based

These questions are intended to serve as ideas and outlines to guide your conversation during the screening and interview process rather than to serve as outright lines of inquiry.

(Note: Many of the personal questions are best suited for in-home care. Most of the job-related questions can offer guidance for most childcare arrangements.)

EHRICH-ROSS INTERVIEW QUESTIONS

Job Related: These questions are applicable to all childcare arrangements except as noted.

- What are your feelings about children?
- Why do/did you choose to be a caregiver?
- How did you find the job at this center?
- How long have you worked here? In this profession?
- How does this center compare to others in the area?
- How and when did your interest in this profession develop?
- Describe how you would spend a typical day with our children.
  - ➤ Good weather/bad weather?
  - ➤ Activities?
- What do you think are the three most important things for a child?

- How do you promote certain types of behavior?
- How do you believe that young children should be disciplined? Older children?
  - ➤ Minor versus major infraction?
  - ➤ Define "well behaved."

(Note: The following questions are oriented for the in-home caregiver.)
- Tell us about your previous childcare experiences.
  - ➤ Ages/genders of children.
  - ➤ What were your responsibilities?
  - ➤ What activities did you do while watching the children?
  - ➤ Have you ever spent a full day alone watching children?
  - ➤ Have you ever baby-sat overnight?
  - ➤ Have you ever driven the children somewhere as part of your job?
  - ➤ Driving record and experience (city driving)?
  - ➤ What were your favorite parts of those jobs?
  - ➤ What were your least favorite parts?
- Why did you decide to attend nanny school? (or get a childcare certificate, etc.?)
  - ➤ What are your impressions of the school and the program?
  - ➤ What is/was your living situation at school? How do you feel about it?
  - ➤ What do/did you do with your free time at night? On weekends?
- What other types of jobs have you held (apart from childcare)?
  - ➤ Responsibilities? Length of employment?
  - ➤ What did you find most enjoyable? Dislike the most?
- Have you ever lived away from home before?
  - ➤ Circumstances?
  - ➤ How long?
  - ➤ Have you ever been to our part of the country/state? What are your impressions?

- Are you working now? Why are you thinking about leaving? May we talk with your current employer for a reference?
- How long would you like to stay in one childcare position?
- Why are you interested in the position we are offering?
- What are you looking for generally in a nanny position?
  - ➤ Children? Family? Work environment? Job content? Benefits?
- How do you feel about moving into a new home?
- Our job requires grocery shopping, starting dinner, and some errands. How do you feel about this?
- What questions do you have for us?
  - ➤ Children? Family? Town? State?

Personal: These are best suited for in-home caregivers.

- Tell us about yourself.
  - ➤ Personality: active/happy-sad/outgoing-quiet
  - ➤ Creativity
  - ➤ Flexibility
  - ➤ Neat-sloppy
  - ➤ How do you handle stress?
  - ➤ Best time of day?
- Describe your sense of humor. What do you think is funny?
- Do you have any hobbies or special interests that you presently pursue?
- What do you do for fun in your free time?
  - ➤ TV? Read? Phone? Exercise? Shopping? Church? Classes? Hobbies?
  - ➤ Do you have a boyfriend or any very close friends?
  - ➤ What are some of your favorite books/movies/TV shows?
- Describe yourself as a close friend would describe you.
- Describe yourself as someone who dislikes you might.

- How would your family (siblings/parents) describe you?
- Tell us about when you were a child.
  - Relationship with parents?
  - Relationship with sisters? Brothers? Other relatives?
  - Happiest memory?
  - Saddest memory?
  - Favorite activities? Books? TV/movies? Music?
  - Tell us about school. Grades? Activities? Awards?
- What was your hometown, your neighborhood, and your home like?
- When you misbehaved, how did your mother handle it? Father?
  - How often were you physically disciplined?
  - How did you feel about the way that you were disciplined?
  - Is there anything that you would change?
- What is your own philosophy on discipline?
- Did you have a caregiver or go to day care when you were growing up? What did you think of the experience?
- What condition is your health?
  - Allergies/asthma/cramps/migraines/other illness or conditions?
  - Have you ever been hospitalized or treated for a major illness?
  - Have you ever received counseling?
  - What do you do to take care of yourself?
- How do you feel about moving to another part of the country? How does your family feel about it?
- How do you think you will spend your free time? Evenings? Weekends?
- What reservations do you have about our position?

How would you handle this childcare situation?
(These questions are suitable for all caregivers and arrangements.)

- Adam (the baby) wants to feed himself but he is very messy.
- Sam is playing outside and doesn't want to come in for the next activity.
- Adam wants to try to climb on the high bars of the jungle gym at the playground.
- Sam and Adam are fighting over a toy.
- You walk into the room and see that Sam is playing with an electrical outlet. He is upset that you caught him.
- Adam won't eat the snack or lunch you prepared for him; he wants a cookie/banana and yogurt/ice cream instead.
- Sam and Adam find a mud puddle in the yard and start to play together in it.
- Sam wants to go out to play and you tell him no because it is too cold. He has a tantrum.
- Sam and another child always seem to be getting into skirmishes.
- Adam refuses to go along with the planned activity on the schedule (e.g., nap time, outside play, etc.).

Reference Questions for Centers and Individuals

Center Reference Questions

Note: Remember to verify that this is a legitimate reference by confirming some of the background facts you were given by the center.

1. How did you first learn of the center? What attracted you to the center initially? What other centers did you consider? Why did you end up choosing this center?
2. How did you feel about the quality of the care your child received? The quality of the facilities? How did you feel about the childcare providers?
3. What are the strengths of the center's program? What do you think are the three biggest weaknesses of the program?
4. What aspect of the center or its staff would you have changed? What suggestions can you offer for improvements at the center?
5. Why did your child stop attending the center? (Check the facts.) Were there any factors that, if different, would have led you to reconsider your decision? What were they?
6. Would you enroll your child at the center again? Why?
7. Would you recommend the center to your best friend or a close relative?
8. Do you have anything else to add or bits of advice?

Individual Caregiver Reference Questions

Note: These questions pertain to *individual* caregivers who would work in your home. You can also use these for family day care if you feel it is helpful. Your own questions may not be quite as detailed. That is fine; this list is meant to be a source of ideas, not an exhaustive compilation. Remember to take the time to verify that this is a legitimate reference.

General Reference
➤ How do you know the candidate?
➤ Describe her to me.
➤ What are her best qualities?
➤ What areas do you feel need improvement?
➤ Rate on a scale of 1–10 (10 is highest):
  ➤ Work ethic?
  ➤ Flexibility?
  ➤ Maturity?
  ➤ Common sense?
  ➤ Sense of humor?
  ➤ Disposition?
  ➤ Self-confidence?

Childcare Reference
➤ What sorts of activities did she do with your children?
➤ What do your children think of her?
➤ Did she ever have to:
  ➤ drive your children anywhere?
  ➤ watch them overnight?
  ➤ prepare meals?
  ➤ handle a disruption of plans (e.g., expected to do something but the weather was bad)?
  ➤ handle an emergency?
➤ How much supervision did you have to provide?
➤ Would you hire her again for your job? (This is the *best* question.)

➤ Would you recommend her for a nanny position? Do you have any reservations?

Other Work Reference
➤ Length of employment?
➤ Job requirements?
➤ What kind of worker was she? (Prompt? Well groomed? Healthy? Friendly? Professional? etc.)
➤ Level of responsibility given?
➤ Willingness to accept responsibility? (Did just what was required? More? Less?)
➤ Would you hire her again? Why?
➤ How would you rate her qualifications for our position?

Family/Friend Reference
➤ How long have you known her?
➤ Describe her as a child to me.
➤ Did she become the sort of adult you envisioned she would be?
➤ If she were not related to you, would you choose to be her friend? Why?
➤ How do you feel about her choice of profession?
➤ How do you feel about the prospect of her moving far from home and family for a position?
➤ How do you think she will do being far from home?
➤ Are you generally comfortable or uncomfortable with this situation?
➤ Do you have any questions or concerns for us to respond to?
➤ Would you hire her for this position in your home?
➤ Would you recommend her for this position in our home?
➤ Do you have any reservations?

Sample Contract for Nanny Services
(Simplified Version)

Nanny:

Mary Poppins

Family:

The Smith Family

Employment Period:

July 1, xxxx–June 30, xxxx

Hours and Days of Service:

Monday through Friday from 7:00 A.M. until 6:00 P.M. with additional hours as arranged plus one Saturday evening per month.

Responsibilities:

1. All childcare responsibilities related to the needs of Sam and Adam during the hours and days of service including:
   - interactive play; help with homework
   - proactive arrangement and transportation to activities and appointments including but not limited to weekly

library trips, sporting activities, enrichment programs, etc.
- bathing; laundry; preparing and feeding meals and snacks during the day
- keeping all household common areas, children's rooms, and play areas clean and tidy

2. The following guidelines shall apply at all times:
- no physical discipline
- one hour of educational TV or videos per day and only after chores, bathing, homework and creative play time are completed
- visual supervision of children

3. Other responsibilities include the following:
- grocery shopping and putting away all groceries
- family laundry and folding
- commence preparation of evening meal for family
- doing local errands (e.g., dry cleaners, etc.)

Compensation:

- Weekly salary of $XXX to be paid every Friday.
- Ten days' vacation must be coordinated with our family plans for vacation.
- Six legal paid holidays: New Year's Day, President's Day, Memorial Day, July 4th, Thanksgiving Day, and Christmas Day.
- Use of car for job-related and personal reasons. Note: From time to time, we will need the car; we will try to give you as much notice as possible in these cases. If there is any damage to the car or excessive gas usage or maintenance requirements, you are required to reimburse us for such costs.
- Private bedroom and telephone line. Note: You are responsible for keeping your room clean, paying for any damage or excessive wear to the room or its contents, and for the costs of all toll calls made.

House Rules:

- No smoking in our home or cars, or in front of our children.
- Please let us know if you plan on having guests visit you in our home.
- No food or beverages to be consumed outside of the kitchen.
- No personal calls or visits while on duty.

Termination of Agreement:

This agreement may be terminated by either party by providing four weeks' notice to the other. Recession can take place in a lesser period by mutual consent or if the terms of this contract are violated. This agreement may be amended by mutual consent only.

The undersigned agree to the terms, duties, and schedule as described above.

_____

Employee   Date

_____

Employer   Date

Sample Contract for Nanny Services
(Detailed Version)

Nanny:

Mary Poppins

Family:

The Smith Family

The following agreement describes the expected schedule, duties to be performed, living accommodations, house rules, salary, duration of employment, and other miscellaneous items associated with the employment of Mary Poppins as a nanny for the Smith family.

EMPLOYMENT TERM

Employee will begin work on July 1, xxxx, for a period of one year.

WORK SCHEDULE

The expected working hours are 7:00 A.M. to 6:00 P.M. Monday through Friday, plus one Saturday evening monthly (for four to five hours) with all other Saturdays, every Sunday, prearranged vacation days, and specified legal holidays off. In addition, we require that you spend approximately thirty minutes with us on the weekend at a mutually agreeable time (usually Sunday evening) so that we can go over the schedule for the upcoming week. We expect your cooperation and flexibility regarding this schedule in the case of an emergency or extenuating circumstances. Any significant extra working hours will be prearranged to the extent possible and be compensated appropriately.

DUTIES AND RESPONSIBILITIES

The employee will be expected to perform the following duties:

Childcare:

- playing with the children;
- proactively planning recreational activities (e.g., play dates, arts-and-crafts projects, outings to parks/library/pool, special events, etc.) on a weekly basis and discussing these plans in advance with the parents;
- planning, participating in and supervising at least two hours of outdoor play for the children every day (except in severe weather conditions) in addition to any other activities that may take the children out of the house. **The children must be supervised and in sight at all times when outside of our home even if they are in the backyard;**
- proactively talk to the children's teachers about school activities and how the children are doing so that we can be kept up-to-date on what is happening there;
- waking the children in the morning, dressing them, etc., in preparation for the day;
- bathing the children every evening before dinner;
- preparing and serving nutritious meals and snacks and cleaning up afterward (including putting dishes in dish-

washer, washing pots, etc., running and/or emptying the dishwasher as needed, wiping up counter and table, sweeping floor [if needed], returning food and dishes/utensils to proper place, etc.). The children are to eat all meals and snacks served at home while seated in the kitchen or at the table on the deck;

- driving the children to and from school, scheduled activities and appointments, and on outings;
- keeping children's bedrooms, playroom, and bathroom clean and organized (e.g., pick up and organize toys, make beds); putting away outdoor toys (bikes, riding toys, basketballs, etc.);
- accompanying the children to library, parties, special events, medical appointments, pool, etc., when necessary and/or if requested;
- supervising all activities in and out of the home while caring for the children (including outdoor play, play dates at our home—or out if requested to stay by child), etc.;
- appropriately disciplining the children in our absence. Good judgment and common sense work well in most situations. We prefer use of positive reinforcement and time-out with variations thereon. **Under no circumstances may physical discipline be used;**
- the children are permitted to watch up to an average total of one hour of TV or videos daily. Less is better. The only permitted TV station is PBS (Channel 13) and the only permitted videos are those we own or those that are rented of an educational and nonviolent nature (e.g., Dr. Seuss, Charlie Brown, etc.);
- responding flexibly to the needs of the children and serving as a positive role model.

Other Responsibilities:

- doing weekly grocery shopping for household and putting away the groceries;

- doing laundry for the children and parents; mending children's clothing as needed; folding and putting away the children's clothing, folding parent's clothing;
- running local errands with the children such as buying birthday gifts, dropping off/picking up dry cleaning, etc.;
- taking in mail (to be left on the kitchen counter) and taking family telephone messages;
- starting preparation of dinner in the evening including tasks such as making a salad, heating a casserole, setting the table, etc. The meals will be planned in advance in consultation with the family;
- joining in family efforts to keep the home tidy between visits from the cleaning lady.

LIVING ARRANGEMENTS

Bedroom:

Employee will have own fully furnished private bedroom on the third floor with air-conditioning and own thermostat. Please do not heat or cool the room when you are not in it (i.e., working hours or if out on the weekend). *The nanny is also responsible for keeping her own room clean and organized.*

A telephone with a separate line and an answering machine will be provided for personal calls during your free time. *The nanny is responsible for paying for all calls made on this line.*

Towels and sheets will be washed on a weekly basis by the cleaning lady provided they are left by the washing machine in the morning prior to her arrival. Changing bed linens, doing personal laundry, dusting and all other cleaning of the room is the full responsibility of the nanny.

You may entertain one friend in your room although we prefer that visits end once children are in bed due to the layout of the house; small groups of friends may be entertained in the den (see below).

Eating and drinking are not permitted in your room.

In the event that you cause any damage to the room or its contents (or elsewhere in our home), you are fully responsible for paying for the repairs.

Kitchen and Meals:

Our kitchen is yours. We are happy to have you join us for meals or you may prepare your own, whichever you prefer. Please let us know your plans, however, so we can cook accordingly. If you wish to serve refreshments or meals to a guest(s), please let us know in advance, depending on the situation, you may be requested to purchase your supplies. Please consume all food and beverage in the kitchen.

Den/Playroom:

When the den is not being used by the children, the employee may entertain a small group (up to three) of her guests there. We ask that you let us know in advance if you would like to have guests visit.

Car:

The employee will have use of the station wagon for professional use; personal use is a privilege to be earned with safe and responsible driving and respect for the car as our property. The car will be available for personal use subject to our advance approval. You may not drive the car for long distances (more than ten miles) without our prior consent, nor may you drive into Manhattan, any of the New York boroughs, or to other highly trafficked areas (Hoboken, etc.).

You are expected to treat our car as carefully as you would your own property by driving safely at all times and keeping it clean with regular car washes and interior vacuuming. We will pay for gas as it relates to professional use and for regular maintenance; in cases when personal use has resulted in excessive wear and tear or gas consumption, you are responsible for these costs. If the employee receives a ticket or has an accident in which she is at fault, she is responsible for paying any costs incurred as a result. **Under no circumstances whatsoever will unsafe driving or drinking and driving be tolerated.**

SALARY AND BENEFITS

The employee will be paid $XXX every Friday after completing the work week. You may receive up to $XXX as an educational stipend for classes that we mutually agree are related to job responsibilities. This will be paid when you complete the class with a passing grade.

There are ten vacation/personal days. We require that the employee coordinate *all* vacation plans with those of our family. No vacation may be taken in the first four months of employment unless it is to coordinate with our vacation. From time to time, the employee will be invited to join our family on vacation. If you work during this vacation, the compensation arrangement shall be negotiated and agreed upon before the holiday commences.

There are six legal paid holidays: New Year's Day, President's Day, Memorial Day, July 4th, Thanksgiving Day, and Christmas Day. We will be inviting you to join us in celebrating some of the major holidays with our family and hope that you will join us.

HOUSE RULES

We expect the employee to come home at a respectable hour in the evening so as to not interfere with job-related duties the next day. On the weekends or holidays, if you expect to be out very late or not return that evening, kindly let us know in advance so we do not worry needlessly.

Friends may visit with our prior approval. We ask that the employee not have a guest in her own room once any family member is getting ready for bed and also that she limit herself to one guest in the room at a time (unless this is discussed with and agreed to by us in advance). We prefer that the employee not entertain a male guest in her room. Overnight guests are not allowed without our prior approval.

We respect each other's privacy and rights. Simple courtesies, such as knocking and waiting for a reply before opening a door, emptying the dishwasher or kitchen garbage, keeping the common rooms tidy and cleaning up after oneself, are practiced and appreciated in our home. We also ask that you respect our family's privacy by not discussing with your own friends or family any personal matters that may arise in our private lives.

All food and beverages are to be consumed in the kitchen or on the deck.

Smoking is not permitted in our home or car by anyone, guest or resident.

Personal telephone calls may not be made or accepted while on duty except in an emergency.

TERMINATION OF AGREEMENT

This agreement may be terminated by either party by providing four weeks' notice to the other. Recession can take place in a lesser period by mutual consent or if the terms of this contract are violated. This agreement may be amended by mutual consent only.

The undersigned agree to the terms, duties, and schedule as described above.

Employee   Date

Employer   Date

Medical Emergency Letter

Caregiver should carry one copy in purse and have one in the house. If letter is more than one page long, STAPLE all the pages together.

Your address
Re: List all your children by full name

To Whom It May Concern:
   CAREGIVER NAME has my permission to authorize appropriate emergency medical treatment for my children, CHILD NAME and CHILD NAME, in the event that my husband or I or any other authorized emergency contacts (below) cannot be reached in a timely manner.
   Our pediatrician is Dr. ABC (PHONE and ADDRESS) and our dentist is Dr. XYZ (PHONE and ADDRESS). CHILD NAME has the following medical conditions you should note: (include and complete if applicable with all necessary details).
   I accept financial responsibility for any such emergency treatment. Below is my insurance information.

Sincerely,
YOUR SIGNATURE
Print your name

Emergency contacts
Your name: work and home phone number
Spouse name: work and home phone number
Other names: work and home phone number (Put one or two, such as a grandparent or best friend.)

Insurance Info
(Photocopy of your card or note name of insurer, telephone number, policy number, etc.)

Childcare Search and Information Resources

American Council of Nanny Schools (ACNS)
Joy Shelton
c/o Delta College
University Center, MI 48710
Phone: 517–686–9417
Fax: 517–686–8736
Compiles information on nanny training programs and placement agencies. Can provide literature.

Child Care Action Campaign (CCAC)
330 7th Ave., 17th Floor
New York, NY 10001
E-mail: ccacgen@aol.com
Offers free literature on childcare, including information on how to look for it and how to advocate for it in your community or at your place of employment.

Child Care Aware
Phone: 1–800–424–2246
Web site: www.yourchild.yahoo.com
A corporate-sponsored information resource that offers community childcare referral and resource agencies in your locality as well as informational brochures on childcare issues.

I Am Your Child
Phone: 1–888–447–3400
Web site: www.iamyourchild.org
A national public-awareness campaign (sponsored by the Reiner Foundation) to help parents understand early childhood development issues. Pamphlets, CD-roms, and videos

on this subject as well as on selecting quality childcare are available for free or for a nominal shipping charge.

International Nanny Association (INA)
900 Haddon Ave. #438
Collingswood, NJ 08108–2101
Phone: 609–858–0808
Fax: 609–858–2519
Web site: www.nanny.org
Can supply a family package of information regarding nannies. For a fee will also provide a training package that includes a listing of nanny training programs, placement agencies, and special services.

National Association of Child Care Resource and Referral Agencies (NACCRRA)
1319 F St. NW, Suite 606
Washington, D.C. 20004
Phone: 202–393–5501
Fax: 202–393–1109
Web site: www.naccrra.net
Provides comprehensive listing of community-based childcare resource and referral agencies in your area.

National Association for the Education of Young Children (NAEYC)
1509 16th St. NW
Washington, D.C. 20036-1426
Web site: www.naeyc.org
Offers several pamphlets on childcare and early childhood developmental issues. Accredits day-care centers.

National Association for Family and Child Care (NAFCC)
206 6th Ave., Suite 900
Des Moines, IA 50309–4018
Phone: 515–282–8192

Fax: 515–282–9117

Web site: www.nafcc.org

Provides lists of providers who have obtained NAFCC accreditation.

National Child Care Association (NCCA)

1029 Railroad St.

Conyers, GA 30207–5275

Phone: 770–922–8193

Fax: 770–388–7772

Web site: www.nccanet.org

Affiliated with National Early Childhood Program Accreditation (NECPA) at 1–800–505–9878. Provides listing of providers who have earned accreditation of its affiliate, NECPA.

Bold type denotes charts. Italicized type denotes sample letters.